D1485033

youth netball

drills

age **12** to **16**

Also available from A & C Black

101 Youth Football Drills – Age 7–11
3rd edition
Malcolm Cook

101 Youth Football Drills – Age 12–16
3rd edition
Malcolm Cook

101 Youth Netball Drills – Age 7–11
2nd edition
Anna and Chris Sheryn

101 Youth Hockey Drills
2nd edition
Stuart Dempster and Dennis Hay

anna and chris sheryn

youth netball

drills

age **12** to **16**

SECOND EDITION

B L O O M S B U R Y
LONDON • NEW DELHI • NEW YORK • SYDNEY

Published in 2005 and 2010 by A&C Black Publishers Ltd

Reprinted by Bloomsbury Publishing Plc
50 Bedford Square, London, WC1B 3DP
www.bloomsbury.com

Bloomsbury is a trademark of Bloomsbury Publishing Plc

First edition 2005
Second edition 2010, reprinted 2014

ISBN 978 14081 9995 4

Acknowledgements
Cover photograph by Getty Images
Textual illustrations by Q2A Solutions and Mark Silver
All photographs courtesy of Getty Images

Typeset in 10/12pt DIN regular
Printed and Bound in Great Britain by CPI Group (UK) Ltd, Croydon, CR0 4YY

CONTENTS

ACKNOWLEDGEMENTS

Thank you to my enthusiastic guinea pigs at Ashgate Netball Squad and all the children at Cowling Primary School Netball Club. Also, thank you to all those coaches of netball training sessions I have enjoyed over the years, from school to county.

INTRODUCTION

Netball is a fantastic, competitive team sport played by over one million women and girls each week in the UK alone! Accessible to all ages and abilities, netball is a skilful, physical, athletic game that provides opportunities for both social, fun activity as well as competing at the highest levels.

The aim of this book is to give coaches, teachers and parents a resource to construct effective drill sessions to introduce young players to netball. It is important for all netballers to be able to consistently perform the simple things well and learning good habits at the start will provide a good foundation for any young player. The drills included are designed to introduce the basic skills and concepts and include the common themes of movement, core passing and catching skills. Some drills therefore cover the same skill elements in a slightly different way, helping to add some variety to keep the sessions interesting – remember the key objective of any practice session is to ensure the players want to come back for the next one. Their experience in these early years can determine whether they continue to play (at any level) into adult life, and also has the potential to influence their view of sport in general; this can be seen as an enormous responsibility or a real opportunity! It can certainly provide some wonderful rewards.

All players, and in particular young players, need to have fun and enjoy their netball, which includes their training; it is important not to burden them with abstract concepts or complicated tactics that they will not understand or be able to perform and can potentially erode their confidence. For this reason there is a strong sense of fun running through all the drills and the opportunity to introduce a little imagination – if they can learn and not notice they are doing so, whilst enjoying themselves, you have succeeded.

KEY TO DIAGRAMS

GS   Goal Shooter

GA   Goal Attack

WA   Wing Attack

C   Centre

WD   Wing Defence

GD   Goal Defence

GK   Goal Keeper

△   cones

- - - - - - ➤   movement of ball

———————➤   movement of player

SESSION GUIDELINES

buying in

It is important that the players are well aware of the objectives behind each activity. This 'buying in' is doubly important when explaining the more abstract and complex drills, as unless the players understand why they are being asked to do something, they will not totally engage in the activity. This is especially vital for young players, who will not be experienced enough to understand why all this running about is going to help their game.

When you introduce a drill, ensure that everyone is very clear on:

- the skill they are practising: 'this drill focuses on running to receive a pass head-on'
- why it is an important skill: 'you can use this skill to drive towards the pass in a game and therefore beat your marker to the ball'
- what a good job looks like: 'get your hands up early as you run, then cushion the ball in as you take the pass; start slowly for the first few passes, then gradually build up speed and see what your limits are'
- mistakes are positive: practice and drills are the place to try things out. For example, 'How far can you hang back from your marker (to draw the pass) and still manage to get the interception?' Until players 'fail', they cannot measure their limits and then work to improve on them. Always congratulate players who are trying as well as those who succeed.

building drills

When you are introducing complex drills to groups of players, always explain each element separately so that everyone is clear about what they have to do before they start. By flooding the group with information, you run the risk of the drill becoming disorganised or falling apart. For example, if the drill involves a run–receive–land–pass sequence, demonstrate and describe the run and land only at first so that everyone can see and understand what a good job looks like. Only add the next element when the basics are spot on. There is absolutely no point in introducing a ball to a drill if the running and landing principle is not understood.

quality before quantity

Building an environment of excellence can be achieved without becoming boring. Just be very clear and concise about the skills you are about to practise and then concentrate on quality of execution at all times. Do not be drawn into lengthy drills that test stamina and reduce quality of play – short, sharp, top-quality drills will ensure that top-quality play is ingrained.

Remember: 'Practice does not make perfect; it makes permanent.' If sloppiness is part of the training regime, it will become ingrained in performances.

the learning curve

The development of a skill during a group practice will not follow a straight line. It is usual for awareness and concentration initially to be high, and for skills to develop at a corresponding rate. However, as the drill progresses concentration levels will fall and therefore so will players' accuracy. If this is allowed to continue unchecked by the coach, competency levels will suffer.

To address this issue, coaches must constantly be aware of the pattern of the players' concentration levels and take time to rest their minds and bodies. Stop the drill, re-communicate the objective and the skills involved and then, once the players are rested and ready – both mentally and physically – start again. In this way the inevitable decline in competency can be arrested and the development curve can be edged upwards.

confidence

When boys encounter problems they are likely to blame the ball, the weather, the passer – anything but themselves. With girls, the first port of call tends to be their own performance. This means that the coach must ensure that confidence is not undermined by progressing drills too quickly for the ability of the players. Instead, use drills that provide initial success, and progress slowly. Always focus on what has gone right and not on perceived failures.

communication

In any sport, on most training nights you will see a coach struggling to form young players into pre-drill formations. Instructions such as 'Get into a circle' or 'I need two staggered lines' result in formations that owe more to a stage farce than a netball session. This leads to exasperated coaches, confused players and wasted time.

Never fear – here are some tips to help you overcome some common problems.

Watch your language

I know an excellent tennis coach who, when working with a group of 6–8-year-olds, told them to 'Stand in the tramlines'. I mentioned to him afterwards that the reason that not all of them responded was that many of them had no idea what a tramline was, and even less idea which area of the court he was talking about.

Try at all times to take account of the age and experience of your players before you speak. Avoid jargon like the plague, explain what you mean and constantly question and re-evaluate your use of language. If you want to test yourself, ask a non-netballer to watch a session and keep a list of all the terms that they do not understand. Have a look at the list and then ask yourself what you really meant!

'Get into pairs/groups of three etc.'

You can pair up older players by asking everyone to put their hands in the air and keep them there until they have a partner. In this way it is easier for everyone to see who remains.

'Make a circle'

Ask a group of players (of almost any age) to form a circle, and what you get will likely resemble a football crowd. A good way to achieve an evenly spaced circle is to ask all the players to hold hands and then slowly walk backwards as far as they can without letting go. You will be left with an evenly spaced circle.

'Form a staggered line'

In a number of the drills in this book you will need the players to form two parallel lines in a zigzag formation. This, again, can be a real struggle. The easy way to do this is in four steps:

1 Ask the players to form a single line and then hold hands.
2 Spread them out until they can only just hold onto each other – they will then be evenly spaced.
3 Number alternate players one and two – 'One, two, one, two' etc.
4 All number ones stand still. All number twos walk out to form the second line. When both lines turn to face each other, they will form the perfect 'zigzag'.

warming up

A 'warm-up' is necessary to prepare the body for exercise, but children need less warm-up time than adults and contrary to traditional wisdom, there is no evidence that stretching before exercise improves performance or reduces the risk of injury. Instead, stretches should be performed after exercise.

Whilst children need less warming up, introducing this as part of a training session is a good habit to get them into. It is also a good way to get them engaged and focused on netball, rather than whatever they were doing before! It helps to get them ready for the rest of the session. For youngsters it is important to make the warm-up fun and varied – keep it moving so they don't get bored. Don't strive for perfection – use a little imagination and they will join in with enthusiasm.

A warm-up should consist of similar movements to the exercises players are about to perform. There is no point running around the court for 10 minutes if you are then going to perform a series of sprints or jumps. Think about the range of movements that you are preparing the players for and gradually build up the intensity from gentle warm-up to near-performance level.

Be careful not to warm up for too long to avoid using up energy that should be reserved for playing. Players will need to sweat a little, but shouldn't be fatigued by the warm-up. A good rule of thumb is to elevate the heart rate to the extent that players are sweating lightly and are mildly out of breath.

warming down

This tends to be a much ignored area of coaching sessions and as mentioned above, the warm down is the place to work on flexibility. Children have a natural flexibility and whilst muscle fatigue and stiffness are not likely to be a major issue for the young player, awareness of warming down is again a good habit to get them into.

If stretches are carried out consistently during a warm down this can avoid muscle stiffness and soreness in the days following matches; more important for older players.

Structure the warm down to target any specific areas of the body that have been worked during the session, for example, if you have included lots of jumping drills make sure the warm down includes some stretches for the legs (such as calf and hamstring stretches).

drill categories

The drills in this book are divided into the following categories:

1 Warming up
2 Strength and balance
3 Ball skills (passing and catching)
4 Movement and footwork
5 Attacking and defending
6 Shooting
7 Conditioned games
8 Warming down

Some of the drills are basic and introduce skills and techniques for young and inexperienced players, others are more advanced and should only be selected for more confident and experienced players. You can select drills from across the sections to make up a varied and interesting session.

Whilst variety helps keep players and coaches interested some of the basic skills take time to learn and there is no harm in revisiting drills, or having a set routine as part of the warm-up session. We all have favourites and as long as there is a mix of basic skill levels and activity-based drills within a session, everyone should have some fun whilst they are learning.

session structure

There are as many ways to compile a session as there are coaches. There are some basic guidelines that will help a session make sense for players and coaches. The length of time for a training session will vary depending on the age of the players – an hour session is a long time for very young players to concentrate and be physically active. A 45 minute session would be better. It is good to finish a session in a well-structured, controlled way rather than it fizzle out because players have lost interest or are too tired.

A key element to your session for this age group is to interest them enough to come back for the next session.

A golden rule: always ensure the session ends on a positive note, reinforcing the technique and skill covered in the session.

Typical session structure:

At the beginning let players know what you will be working on in the session. For young, inexperienced players it is good to pick one type of skill or new technique and concentrate on that throughout – don't confuse them with trying to introduce too many things at once. (This goes for all ages at times!)

As the sessions progress and your group becomes more confident, reminders of skills covered in previous sessions are good. Remember, build on skills slowly to improve confidence, encourage quality and instil good habits.

Warm-up (maximum 10 minutes)

The aim is to get them ready for the session and focused on you and netball. Include drills that introduce some basic movement techniques and dynamic stretching.

With this age group it is appropriate to introduce some strength work and whilst we focus on this in the strength and balance drills, it is a good idea to include these at the beginning of the training session or at the end just before the warm-down. Include two or three of the strength and balance drills as part of the warm-up; make sure players have completed some basic warm-up drills first so that they are warm and their muscles have been stretched.

Aim to finish this section with a game-based activity from the warm-up drills to add a fun element.

Drills (maximum 20 minutes)

Select the drills depending on the objective for the session. In some cases the drills provide a natural progression and it will be clear which drills to use first. Only progress the drills if there are clear indications that the players are coping and developing good technique.

Some people will pick up the drills more easily than others; allow time to be able to explain the drill and what you want them to do and to demonstrate the technique so they can see a good example first. Be prepared to let them try out the drill and then reset your expectations of what they need to do if necessary – remember: look for quality.

Be careful not to 'over drill' a technique – you don't want them to get bored and frustrated. There is no harm in coming back to a drill at a later stage if players are not achieving the quality you are looking for. It helps to have a couple of reserve drills up your sleeve to use at short notice if a drill is not working well – this is particularly useful when introducing some of the more complicated drills that require more concentration and co-ordination.

Play netball (minimum 10 minutes)

Players of all ages have one thing in common – they prefer playing to practising! Make sure they get the chance to play netball in every session, even if only for a short time.

This can be as part of a conditioned game to help introduce a skill or technique into a game situation, or as a game scenario to practise a specific move or sequence, such as a centre pass.

Keep players moving and changing in if you have extra numbers. Encourage observers to help watch out for good skills and give lots of praise for successes and players trying hard. It is a good idea to set targets for players within the game other than scoring goals – goal scoring can be seen as the most important thing for young players and they may feel left out if not playing a shooting position. Set them targets of number of passes, interceptions, centre passes etc., whatever works for the group and you!

A sense of humour on court is essential, not only to help keep the coach sane, but it can also remove tension that can make players less inclined to try hard and risk making a mistake. Enjoy it and have fun!

Warm down (5 minutes)

Don't miss this bit out! Whilst young players have less need for stretching as their natural flexibility is better than in adults, this gives you the chance to reaffirm the skill/ objective of the session and finish on a high note.

England's Sara Bayman marking Australia's Madison Browne, trying to prevent an easy pass into the goal circle (World Series 2009).

WARMING UP

As previously mentioned, the warm-up is an important part of the session. While there is no evidence to prove that a warm-up aids performance or helps to avoid injuries, experience tells us that a relevant and focused warm-up prepares both mind and body for the practice. The warm-up is also an opportunity for the players to weigh up a new coach, so if you are new to the group make sure that your session is well planned, clear, well delivered and, above all, fun!

Contrary to traditional wisdom, the warm-up is not the place to improve flexibility (save this for the warm-down when the muscles are warm). The warm-up should be controlled and replicate the types of activities that you will be focusing on in the body of the session. So, three times around the court then touch your toes is not really what we are after!

The following drills provide some ideas for warming up with and without the ball, including some basic movement and mobility exercises, and some game-based activities. It doesn't matter how old they are, always follow the same rule – build speed and intensity gradually and focus on quality of movement. Finish the warm-up with a game-based activity and they should be raring to go!

drill 1 *shuttles*

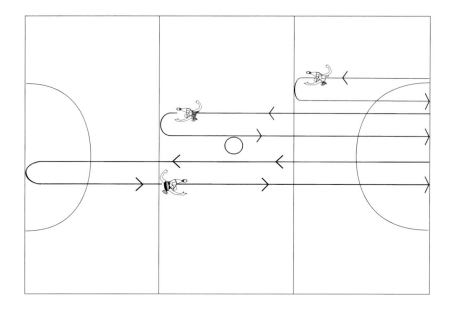

Objective: To warm up the body and practise pushing off on one foot to change direction and keep movement balanced.

Equipment: The whole length of the court.

Description: Players line up along the baseline. On the coach's whistle, the players jog to the first third line, then turn to return to the baseline by pushing off on their landing foot and turning their shoulders to transfer the balance of weight and change direction. The players then jog to the second third line and back, then to the other baseline and back, each time performing the same action to turn.

Coaching points: Watch for a tendency to forget to change direction by pushing off on one foot and turning the shoulders, which reduces the player's balance.

Progressions: Jog to the line then sprint back, always keeping a balanced change of direction. Pair up the players and run shuttles in relay. Player 1 jogs or sprints to the third line and back, then player 2 repeats, and so on until the whole court has been covered.

drill 2 fast feet

Objective: To develop foot speed, balance and control of movement.

Equipment: Cones.

Description: Set up a line of cones 5 m away from the sideline. The players stand on the sideline facing the cones then, using very fast feet and tiny steps, move towards the cones. When the players reach the cones they turn and walk slowly back to the sideline and start again. The objective is to complete as many tiny steps in the shortest amount of time possible.

Coaching points: Youngsters will lose concentration and form very quickly and will increase the length of their steps in order to move forwards more quickly. Re-emphasise the 'fast feet and tiny steps' before each start. The race is not to see who moves forwards fastest, but rather who can get the most steps in over the specified distance.

Progression: Try a timed race – who can perform the most steps in 10 seconds?

drill 3 *knees and heels*

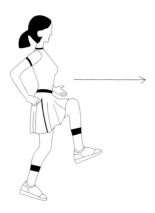

Objective: To warm up and introduce dynamic stretches for quads and glutes.

Equipment: Half a court.

Description: This can be performed in teams depending on numbers. Players line up along the sideline facing into the court area. They jog across the court lifting their knees high as they go. When they reach the other side they turn round and return doing heel flicks. Heel flicks should be done at a slow pace with players flicking their heels up to reach their bottom as they move.

Coaching points: For young players keep this drill short and reduce the space if necessary. The emphasis should be on controlled movements to help stretch out quads and hamstrings while on the move. Movement should be balanced with players maintaining an upright position throughout each movement, using their arms to help with balance. This can be performed as a relay with a group of players on each sideline taking it in turns to complete high knees and heel flicks.

drill 4 *side jumps*

Objective: To improve general agility; to condition the groin muscles (adductors and abductors); to prevent imbalance injuries and stabilise the prime muscle groups.

Equipment: The width of the court.

Description: Split the group into four lines (A, B, C and D), A and B on one side-line and C and D on the other. All players face up the court so they are side on to each other. With good posture, line A side-jumps across the court aiming for height and distance on each jump. Line C then begins the drill, and so on.

Coaching points: Insist on quality at all times. Allow lots of recovery between sets. As players tire there will be a tendency for bodies to sag and for players to twist into a run. Looking backwards to where they came from will help players keep their bodies in the correct position. There is no need for fast forward movements – height and 'hang time' are what you want to see.

Progression: With older players encourage criticism and observation so they become their own coaches. Remind them that form and quality are everything!

drill 5 *high kicks*

Objective: To develop strength and movement skills.

Equipment: Players.

Description: Starting on the sideline, players march out to the centre of the court performing a series of high kicks, clapping their hands under the thigh with each stride. Each leg lift must be as high as possible and the drill must be kept under control. The objective is perfect form, not speed.

Coaching points: Insist on straight legs during this movement. Don't allow the body to curl towards the knee. It doesn't matter how high the straight leg comes as long as the form is perfect. Over a period of time the range of movement will improve and develop.

Progression: Give each player a marker (anything will do – margarine-tub lids are fine). Ask them to stomp out for eight strides, put the marker down and, after walking back to the start, try to reach their marker in fewer strides.

drill 6 *hamstring scoop*

Objective: To warm up and stretch the hamstrings.

Equipment: Half a court.

Description: This can be performed in teams depending on numbers. Players line up along the sideline facing into the court area. Moving at a slow pace across the court players stretch one leg out in front, the leg should be straight with a slight bend in the knee and toes on the floor, the supporting leg should be bent and their weight should be into their bottom to start. Players scoop their arms down towards the toes of their outstretched leg, keeping this as straight as possible as they perform the scoop movement. When they reach the bottom of the scoop they continue lifting their arms above their head and stepping through with the supporting leg so this then becomes the outstretched leg. The scoop is repeated and the player moves across the court stretching alternate legs as they go.

Coaching points: For young players keep this drill short and reduce the space if necessary. The emphasis should be on controlled movements to help stretch out the hamstrings while on the move. Encourage good form throughout.

drill 7 *the lunge*

Objective: To warm up and stretch the hamstrings and glutes.

Equipment: Half a court.

Description: This can be performed in teams depending on numbers. Players line up along the sideline facing into the court area. Moving at a slow pace across the court players stride out with one leg, lunging forwards, keeping their body upright and dropping the back knee to the floor. They stand upright and step out repeating the lunge with the opposite leg.

Coaching points: This should be a slow controlled movement concentrating on the stretch. It is important that players keep their body upright – look for high chests – and the weight does not come forwards over the toes of the lead leg. This puts strain on the knee joint.

drill 8 *footwork patterns*

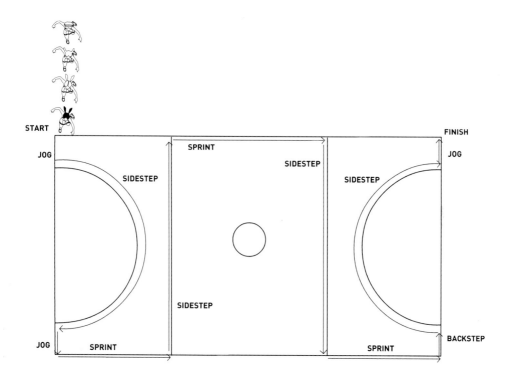

Objective: To practise different footwork steps.

Equipment: The whole court.

Description: Starting at one corner of the baseline players follow each other using the following steps and footwork patterns around the court. Jog along the baseline up to the circle, side step around the circle, then jog the remainder of the baseline. At the sideline change direction and sprint to the third line, sidestep along the third line to the opposite side, then sprint from the third line to the next third line. Sidestep across the court on the third line, sprint to the baseline, backward-steps to the circle line and sidestep around the circle. Jog the remainder of the baseline before finishing in the corner vertically opposite the start.

Coaching points: The aim is to keep the weight balanced, moving forwards with quick changes of direction pushing off from the outside foot.

Progression: Introduce cross steps around the circle edge. Cross steps involve a sideways movement with one foot crossing over the front of the other.

drill 9 *hollow sprints*

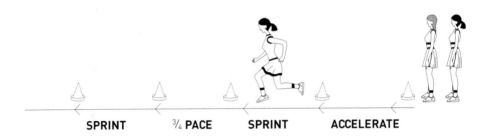

SPRINT   ¾ PACE   SPRINT   ACCELERATE

Objective: To develop a marked change of pace.

Equipment: Five cones.

Description: Divide the court into four 4 x 5 m areas using five cones. Starting at the first cone, players accelerate gently over the first 5 m to the second cone, run at full pace to the third cone, decelerate to three-quarter pace to cone four and hold until the last cone, then accelerate to full pace until the finish line. Walk back to the start slowly to recover.

Coaching points: Here the players are training their bodies to go fast, so they need to perform this drill while they are reasonably fresh. You must also allow plenty of rest between sets to ensure that every set is top quality. If you use this drill when players are tired they will never get the feeling of travelling fast. Tell the players to concentrate on how it feels. When they accelerate, they should drop the hands and lean slightly forwards. This will help to ensure that the power delivered by the legs is propelling the players forwards. Look for changes of speed at the marker points showing control of the pace.

drill 10 zigzag shuttles

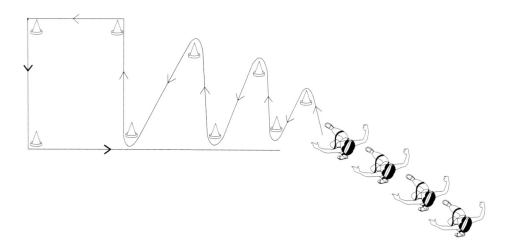

Objective: To warm up by practising sprinting and changing direction.

Equipment: Nine cones.

Description: Set out the cones as shown above over a third of the court. Players line up off court behind the first cone. On the coach's command, the first player jogs to the second cone, turns and sprints to the third cone, turns and jogs to the fourth cone and so on through the grid. When she reaches the penultimate cone, she turns and jogs out to the last cone then walks slowly back to the end of the line and waits her turn to go again.

Coaching points: Let the first runner get through two cones before the next runner sets off. Do not set the cones too far apart as a player will rarely sprint more than about 5 m on court, so anything longer than that in training is not beneficial. Keep the groups large enough that each runner has a good long recovery, but small enough that they do not get cold.

drill 11 _ball thief_

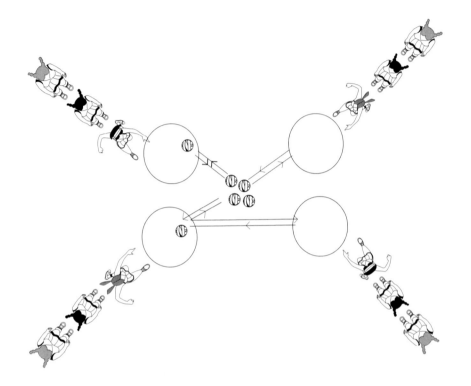

Objective: To develop communication skills and speed.

Equipment: Four hoops (or chalked circles) and six balls.

Description: At each corner of a square (about 5 m wide) place a hoop/circle – these will be 'home base' for each team. Divide the players into four teams and stand them in line, one team behind each base. Place six balls in the centre of the square. On the coach's command, one player from each team runs to the centre to grab one (and only one) ball before returning to base to place it in their hoop/circle. Then the next player in line sets off to grab another ball. Once all the balls have gone from the centre the runners can steal a ball from the other bases. This continues until one team has three balls in their home hoop/circle. If no-one wins within a set time the coach can add another ball to make success a little easier.

Coaching points: Watch out for cheats picking up two balls at a time! Encourage each team to talk to their runner to make her aware of what else is going on around them.

drill 12 *dodge tag*

Objective: To practise dodging skills and improve balanced movement.

Equipment: Players.

Description: The playing area selected should be sufficient to allow players to run around but not so large that it allows full freedom of movement. One third of the court is ideal, or you can reduce the size of the working area using cones. Two players are taggers (T). The rest of the players must dodge out of their way and avoid being tagged. Players who have been tagged must stand still, creating barriers for the other players to dodge around.

Coaching points: Encourage players to make a definite dodge move to avoid the obstacles. Look for quick changes of direction, pushing off on the outside foot and using hips and shoulders to help keep balanced. All footwork should be balanced and controlled.

Progression: Reduce the size of the playing area and increase the number of taggers.

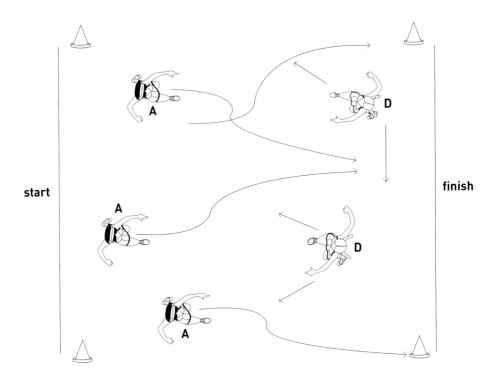

Objective: To warm up by running, dodging and reacting to other players.

Equipment: Four cones.

Description: Two or three defenders (D) stand in the middle of the playing area, the size of which should reflect the age and number of players. On the coach's whistle the other players (attackers or A) try to cross the 'wall' of defenders to reach the other side of the playing area without being tagged. If a player is tagged she joins the defending wall.

Coaching points: Keep the grid small to encourage dodging and sprinting. Ensure players tag below shoulder height for safety.

Progression: Change the footwork patterns of the defending wall and running players. For example, they can run using side steps, and dodge using a push off one foot to change direction.

drill 14 *reaction drill*

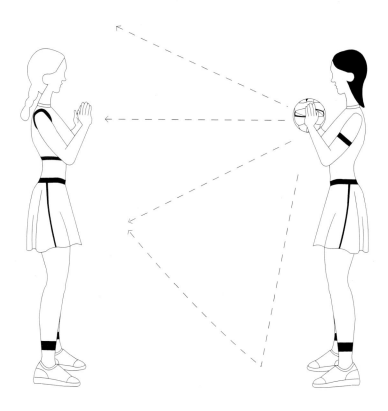

Objective: To encourage good reactions.

Equipment: One ball between two players.

Description: Players face each other approximately 2 m apart. The defender (D) runs quickly on the spot using small steps. The attacker (A) passes or drops the ball in any direction within arm's reach of D. D catches the ball and returns it to A.

Coaching points: All passes should be quick and catch the defender off guard. The defender should aim to stay balanced and in control of her movement and passes. Ensure quality at all times and do not allow wayward passes.

Progression: Forfeits can be included for wayward passes from either person or if the defender stops running.

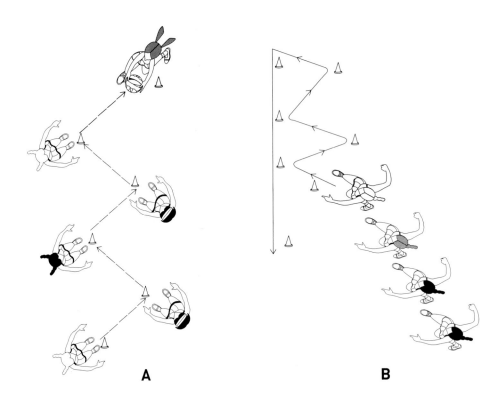

A   **B**

Objective: To warm up the body and practise quick passing and footwork patterns.

Equipment: One ball, cones.

Description: Players are divided into two teams. One team (A) spreads out in a zigzag formation about 3 m apart using half a court. This team passes the ball continuously up and down the zigzag. At the same time, the other team (B) runs in a zigzag over an area covering approximately two-thirds of a court, running one at a time in relay fashion. The passing team counts the number of passes completed in the time it takes all the runners to complete the course. Any pass dropped is not to be added to the total. The teams then reverse roles and compare scores.

Coaching points: Look for accurate, balanced passing. For the runners, movement should be balanced and controlled using quick steps and pushing off on the outside foot.

Progression: Vary the type of pass used. Vary the footwork pattern used.

STRENGTH AND BALANCE

Movement in netball is all about agility, change of speed and direction, and control; all of this requires body strength and balance. Younger and inexperienced players need to learn how to use their body strength to help with their stability and balance, to control their movement and still be able to make a quick, accurate pass.

Core strength is a key element to being able to control balance and momentum; developing strength in the abdominal and back muscles acts as a support for the torso. All players will benefit from developing core strength and at this age some basic routines can be introduced to help do this.

Players who lack core strength will often use incorrect footwork, fall over or fall offside, contact opponents, or be unsteady when receiving a pass which can either reduce the accuracy of their next pass or make the next pass slow – or both!

The drills in this section introduce some basic core strength exercises; it is important to introduce these gradually and focus on good form and technique at all times. In my experience players will find even the simplest of core strength work a challenge so encourage players to master the level that they are capable of before they move onto the next stage of the drill. Even the basic levels will work to improve strength and balance and it is far better to do these well than fail at the higher levels – or worse still, cause an injury!

New Zealand's Casey Williams and Jamaica's Simone Forbes showing their athleticism and the importance of strength and balance in being able to contest the ball (World Series Final 2009).

drill 16 *the stork*

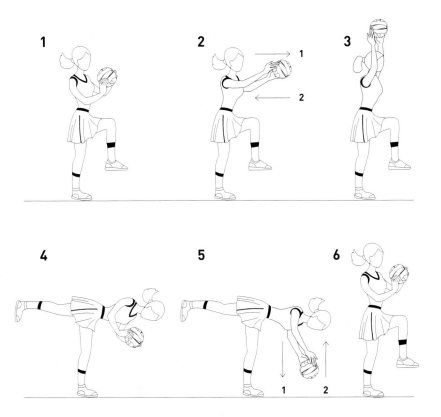

Objective: To improve leg and core strength and balance.

Equipment: One ball per player.

Description: The aim of this drill is to complete all the stages with control and precision – no wobbles! The starting position – the player starts standing on one leg with the other knee held up in front and the ball held close to her chest as shown in (1). The player slowly extends the ball to the front by straightening her arms (2) and back to the starting position and then extends her arms to lift the ball above her head (3) before returning to the starting position. The player then tips forwards from the hips keeping the ball at her chest as shown in (4). Once steady in this position she slowly extends her arms to move the ball towards the floor and returns the ball to her chest – (5). To finish, the player stands back upright into the starting position. These six stages form one repetition. Repeat three times on each leg.

Coaching points: This is a difficult drill to do properly at first and the supporting leg can get tired. Concentrate on one stage at a time and encourage players to only move onto the next stage if they are properly balanced.

drill 17 *the plank*

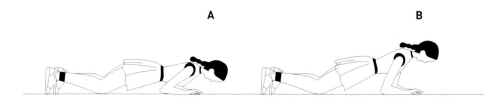

A   B

Objective: To develop core strength.

Equipment: None.

Description: This is an old favourite and performed properly is a good introduction to core strength exercise. The aim is to hold the plank position (A or B depending on ability) for a timed period. Players get into the plank position making sure their body is flat – no sticking up bottoms or sagging hips! Their weight is supported on their elbows and either knees or toes. Hold the position for short periods, i.e. 20 seconds, then rest. Repeat.

Coaching points: Encourage players to hold good form throughout with their body supported in the plank position. It sometimes helps if players imagine they are sucking their tummy button in hard to reach their back. They should keep their neck extended and be facing the floor.

Progression: Increase the time players hold the plank position (up to one minute). Increase the difficulty by supporting the weight on straight arms rather than elbows – ensure the correct body line is maintained at all times.

drill 18 *the side plank*

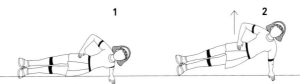

1   2

Objective: To develop core strength, working the oblique abdominal muscles.

Equipment: None.

Description: This is a variation on the plank, targeting the oblique (side) abdominal muscles. The aim is to hold the side plank position at the level achievable depending on ability for a timed period. Players get into the side plank position with their weight supported on bent elbows (hands are forwards), hips and knees, making sure their body is in a straight line – no sticking out bottoms or hips! Players then lift their hips off the floor to support their weight on only their elbows and knees – they need to lift from the waist to do this. The body line must remain straight. Hold the position for short periods, i.e. 20 seconds, then rest. Repeat on the opposite side.

Coaching points: Encourage players to hold good form throughout with their body supported in the side plank position. It sometimes helps if players imagine they are sucking their tummy button in hard to reach their back, and to imagine they are being pulled up by a piece of string around their waist. They should keep their neck extended and relaxed.

Progression: Increase the time players hold the side plank position (up to one minute). Increase the difficulty by supporting the weight on straight arms rather than elbows, and with straight legs instead of having knees bent – ensure the correct body line is maintained at all times.

drill 19 *the press-up*

Objective: To develop core strength.

Equipment: None.

Description: Start in the plank position – the straight body line is supported with straight arms shoulder-width apart and fingers pointing forwards. If this position cannot be supported consistently start in the plank from knees position. Slowly lower the body towards the floor by bending the elbows, hold at the bottom with the body fully supported off the floor for a count of 2 and then straighten the arms to push the back up to the start. Repeat for a set number – building up the repetitions gradually.

Coaching points: This is a progression from the plank and contrary to popular belief is not an arm strength exercise! Core strength is the key to being able to support the body during the press-up action. Perform from the knees if necessary to start and progress to straight legs. Encourage players to try a full press-up – even if they can only do one! Performing this in a slow, controlled movement engages the core muscles. Encourage players to hold good form throughout – no bottoms sticking up or hips sagging down. It sometimes helps if players imagine they are sucking their tummy button in hard to reach their back. They should keep their neck extended and be facing the floor.

drill 20 *standing jump*

Objective: To develop leg strength to help increase jumping height in a game.

Equipment: A wall.

Description: Players stand sideways on to a wall with the arm closest to the wall extended above their head. The aim is to jump as high as they can and touch a point higher up the wall. Repeat five times, then turn round to reach with the opposite arm. This can be performed in pairs with the resting player marking the high point reached in order to measure progression.

Coaching points: This is an explosive exercise from standing. Look for a bend in the knees and a powerful thrust upwards with fingertips reaching for a high point on the wall. Be careful not to over drill – legs will get tired quickly!

drill 21 *ball lunge*

Objective: To develop balance and leg and core strength.

Equipment: One ball per player.

Description: Players start along a sideline holding the ball in one hand above their head. Performing a lunge movement with alternate legs, they move across the court maintaining the ball position at all times. Return with the ball held in the opposite arm.

Coaching points: This is a progression to the lunging movement in the dynamic stretches. For young players it may be appropriate to reduce the working area. Encourage players to hold good form throughout, with the ball held high above their head. Look for the arm extending back slightly behind the head and the elbow should be slightly bent. It is better to do one complete movement perfectly than move across the court without maintaining the ball position or executing sloppy lunges!

drill 22 *the core pass*

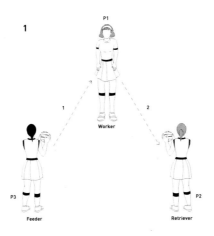

Objective: To develop core strength and balance.

Equipment: Two balls per group of three.

Description: P1 stands in the starting position approximately 3–4 m from P2 and P3. P2 and P3 start with a ball facing P1. P2 feeds a shoulder pass to P1 who catches the ball and returns the pass to P3, maintaining the starting position at all times. As soon as P2 has released the pass to P1, P3 gives her the next ball and looks to P1 to receive a return pass. P3 is a ball retriever to ensure that P2 is able to feed quick passes to P1 and keep the drill moving. Rotate roles after a set number of passes. Make sure all players get to work using both legs as the supporting leg.

Coaching points: Encourage good form and technique at all times with P1 maintaining the starting position – she will need to use her abdominal and back muscles to do this and avoid wobbles. To help, encourage her to suck in her tummy button and pull up her pelvic floor muscles (as if she is trying to stop going for a wee!). To add strength to the pass P1 will also need to use a hip twisting action and this needs to be exaggerated when only using one leg!

Laura Langman (New Zealand) making a quick pass, releasing the ball without stopping or stepping – a key skill of fast-paced netball at the highest level.

MOVEMENT AND FOOTWORK

Good netballers are able to play at a fast pace, change direction, stop and are always ready for the next pass and movement without falling over!

The footwork rule is a basic skill for players to learn and can still be difficult for older players who lack the core strength to control balance and momentum. Keep focusing on the basics and once they are more confident with the idea of landing correctly, controlling their momentum and applying the footwork rule in the majority of situations, coaching can move on to focus on improving their balance, speed and control.

Landing is an important skill to master early; a balanced, controlled landing is the key to being able to make a quick pass, keeps the game moving and also helps to reduce the risk of injury. As players get more experienced, landing on one foot progresses to a running pass, where the ball is caught and released with the player still on the move, speeding up the game and leading to the fast-paced, athletic and attacking netball seen at higher levels.

Another key skill in netball is the art of dodging; a quick, decisive change of direction to out-manoeuvre or wrong-foot a defender and be free to receive a pass or create a space to move into. A dodge is often from a standing position and all players need to be able to master this skill whether an attacker or defender.

Younger, inexperienced players do seem to run around a lot following the ball and lack the control of their movement, change of pace or understanding of the game. This can be the same with this slightly older age group and mastering the dodge is a skill they still need to practise. Even more experienced players have been known to either stand still behind a defender and shout for the ball or run backwards away from the thrower hoping they will lob the ball over the head of their defender. Encouraging a quick dodge and movement towards the thrower to make the pass easier takes time – don't give up, and focus on the basics, building up the complexity slowly as ability and experience develop.

In this chapter, there are drills to practise the basic landing techniques, footwork rule, pivot and dodge. These can be broken down further for very inexperienced players to help them fully understand what is involved and practise good, basic technique from the start. (These introductory drills are available in 101 Youth Netball Drills: Age 7-11). Coaches can select the level of drill to use depending on the experience and ability of their players. The emphasis is still on having fun and the drills are designed to reinforce the skills needed in these key areas through repetition in different situations. The coach should focus on quality throughout.

key coaching points

Landing

1 Players should land with their body upright, feet about shoulder-width apart with feet and knees pointing in the same direction. If a player lands on one foot first the other foot should be brought down quickly with the body weight evenly distributed to form the balanced support needed to make an accurate pass.
2 Players should land with their knees slightly bent; the landing should be cushioned by the ankle, knee and hip joints. Heads should be up, looking at where they are going to make the next pass with shoulders level and relaxed.
3 If players land with their knees over their toes their weight is too far forwards which makes it more difficult to control forward movement. The body weight should be more centred – this is sometimes more difficult for younger players to grasp and coaches need to be patient, encouraging upright landings to enable the players to learn this control.

Dodging

1 Weight should be evenly distributed with feet shoulder-width apart. Heads should be up, looking towards the thrower.
2 The dodge involves a quick movement to one side and a quick transfer of weight and movement to the other side to catch the ball. The first movement should only be one or two quick side steps and then a stop.
3 Encourage players to control their movement and stop by grounding their outside foot and turning on the ball of their foot to move the opposite way, changing the weight to and turning their knees and hips to face the way they are moving.
4 Encourage this quick change of direction by coaching players to push off on their outside foot and transfer their weight to the other foot. This can be difficult for younger players to understand or control.
5 Encourage players to use their arms in a pumping action as they move to help control the movement and accelerate.

Pivoting

1 Encourage a controlled movement, holding the ball close to the body whilst looking up to see where they are going to pass the ball next.
2 The pivot, or rotation should be away from the defender.

golden rules

Balance and control are vital. Controlling the position of the body weight and posture will help players maintain their balance and is the key aspect of good netball skills. Encourage players to maintain a stable position with weight evenly distributed over both feet, heads and eyes up, and feet pointing in the direction they want to throw the ball – all are excellent habits to get into!

It is important for players to practise a balanced landing. Remember that halting a moving body requires a considerable amount of strength and coaches need to be aware this can be difficult for young players, particularly if they are excited and having fun! Keep the drills that involve lots of changes of direction nice and brief so the quality remains high and good habits are practised. There is no harm in rest!

Jumping to catch the ball can help young players to control their forward momentum and land without stepping. It doesn't matter if a player lands on one foot or two, the aim is to be balanced and ready to make the next pass. When on the move and catching the ball it is usual for a player to land on one foot then the other.

drill 23 *the running line*

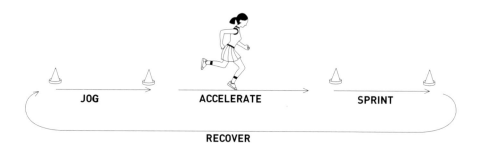

Objective: To introduce the difference between jogging and sprinting, and develop good sprinting technique.

Equipment: Four cones.

Description: Use the cones to mark out three 3 m sets. You will have the start line and then three further cones. The players line up along the start line and jog to the first cone, accelerate gently to the next cone and sprint at full pace to the final cone. Walk back to the start slowly to recover.

Coaching points: Look for a definite change of pace between the jog and the sprint. Encourage players to use their arms to help increase speed. Players need to be reasonably fresh, so allow plenty of rest between sets to ensure that every set is top quality.

drill 24 *jump!*

A

B

Objective: To develop reactions, speed and introduce control of landing.

Equipment: Four different coloured cones.

Description: Set out the cones in a semicircle approximately ½m apart. The distance between the cones can be varied depending on the age and ability of the players. In pairs, player A stands approximately one metre away from the cones in the centre of the semicircle with the four cones in front of her. Player B stands facing her partner. Player B shouts a colour and player A jumps towards that cone and back to the centre as quickly as possible. When she returns to the centre, player B shouts another colour and so on. Swap roles after a short time.

Coaching points: The jumps and landing should be controlled. Encourage players to use their arms to help gain height and distance. When the player lands they should land on two feet and be balanced – no wobbles! Feet should be shoulder-width apart, head up and arms ready as if to receive a pass. Look for a cushioned landing with slightly bent knees. Players should be controlling their movement and be ready to make the second jump a quick reaction.

Objective: To practise quick, controlled changes of direction.

Equipment: Half the court.

Description: The players should space out within the working area. On the coach's whistle they jog in a straight line until they meet either a line or another player. When this happens they must change direction quickly by pushing off one foot and turning their body from the hips and shoulders, using their arms to help. Once they are facing in another direction, they carry on jogging until they meet another obstacle.

Coaching points: The change of direction should be a definite move, quick and controlled. The player is aiming to change direction without losing momentum and speed. It helps to exaggerate the arm and body movement, a bit like a child imitating a steam train!

Progression: Once players are comfortable with jogging, try increasing the pace. Cones placed at random in the working area can be added as extra obstacles.

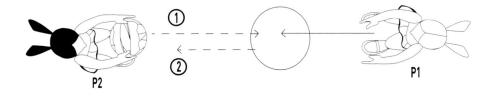

P2   ① ②   P1

Objective: To develop a balanced, controlled two-footed landing technique and practise good timing of the pass to a moving player.

Equipment: One ball per pair, one hoop (or equivalent, a marked spot on the court is sufficient).

Description: The hoop should be placed approximately 2 m from the feeder. Player 1 sprints towards the hoop to receive a chest pass from the feeder as she lands two-footed in the hoop. She then passes the ball back to the feeder with a chest pass and runs backwards to the start. Repeat the drill and swap roles regularly.

Coaching points: Concentrate on one element at a time and if you need to, start with a steady jog first and then introduce the sprint. Look for a good sprinting action, upright and balanced, and a controlled landing, cushioned with the knees bent. The feeder needs to time her pass accurately to reach the space player 1 is sprinting into. Player 1 should be balanced and upright before she returns the pass to the feeder. Encourage good chest pass technique – see ball skills.

Progression: There are an infinite number of progressions to this drill, i.e. vary the type of pass (increase the distance between the landing area and feeder for a shoulder pass), vary the angle of the run for P1, introduce a pivot for P1 when she has received the ball before she returns the pass, add an extra overhead pass from the feeder so P1 receives two passes before returning to the start.

drill 27 *the pivot 1*

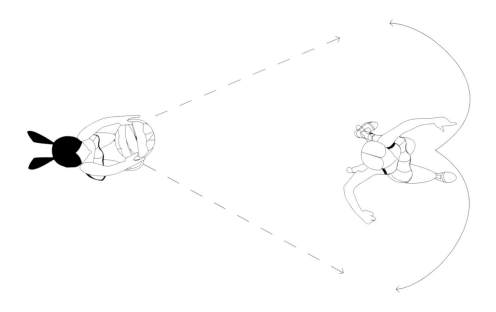

Objective: To practise correct pivoting technique to ensure balance and control.

Equipment: One ball between two players.

Description: Player 1 is working, player 2 is feeding the ball. Player 1 stands with her back to player 2, approximately 3 m away. Player 2 calls 'left' or 'right' to player 1, who pivots to the appropriate side to receive the ball.

Coaching points: Player 1 should start in a balanced position, feet about hip width apart, knees slightly bent and weight on the balls of the feet. Movement should be quick, using little steps, with the hands ready to catch the ball. Players should take turns receiving the ball.

Progression: Vary the type of pass used, for example a high or low ball, bounce pass or pass further away from player 1 so she has to stretch to receive the ball. Player 1 should try to receive the ball in a balanced position rather than at full stretch. The aim is to move the feet quickly; include an extra step if needed to receive the ball.

drill 28 *the pivot 2*

Objective: To practise changing direction by pivoting. Ideal for younger or inexperienced players.

Equipment: One ball between three players.

Description: The three players stand in a line approximately 2 m apart. Player A starts with the ball and passes it to player B. Player B receives the ball and pivots around to pass it to player C. The sequence is repeated in reverse.

Coaching points: Look for an accurate chest pass from all players. Player B should pivot keeping her landing foot in position and should only pass the ball once she is balanced and facing the direction in which she wants the ball to go.

Progression: Vary the type of pass used and speed up the passing.

drill 29 figure 8 drill

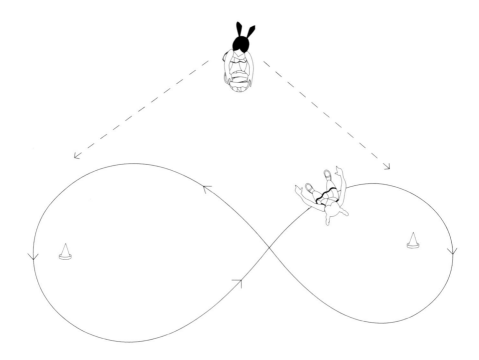

Objective: To improve movement skills and spatial awareness.

Equipment: One ball and two cones between two players.

Description: Set up the cones about 2 m apart. Player 1 stands in front of the two cones. Player 2 runs a figure 8 around the two cones, facing player 1 at all times. In this way player 2 will use a variety of footwork patterns and speeds during the circuit (e.g. quick steps, side steps, cross-overs and so on). At random, player 1 feeds a pass which is received, landed and returned by player 2 before she restarts the circuit.

Coaching points: Watch for players 'following their nose' around the cones. The idea of this drill is that player 2 faces up court and watches the ball at all times. Changes of direction around the cone should be quick and controlled to reduce the time the ball is out of the line of sight and balance must be controlled at all times – if at any time control deteriorates, slow the drill down.

Progression: Move player 1 into different positions to vary the angle of the pass.

drill 30 *the dodge*

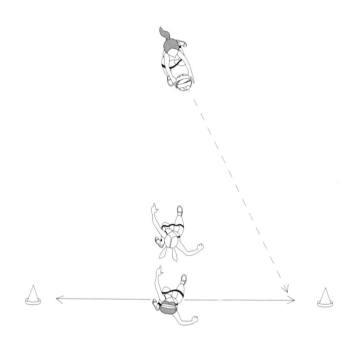

Objective: To practise dodging to get free from a defender and receive a pass.

Equipment: One ball and two cones between three players.

Description: Place the cones approximately 3 m apart. Player A, the attacker stands in between the cones with player B, the defender, standing in front, both facing towards the feeder standing approximately 3m away with the ball. On the coach's whistle, player A makes a quick dodge movement to move away from player B staying within the area marked by the cones to receive a chest pass from the feeder. Player B remains still. Swap roles to allow all players to practise the dodge move and feeding the pass.

Coaching points: This is not a defender practice and is aimed at introducing receiving a pass after a dodge. The defender is only there as a target to 'escape' from. The feeder must time the pass, which must be quick and accurate, to reach the attacker as she moves into the space away from the defender. To help the feeder know where to throw the ball the attacker should indicate (point) to where she will be moving before she makes the dodge.

drill 31 *body control*

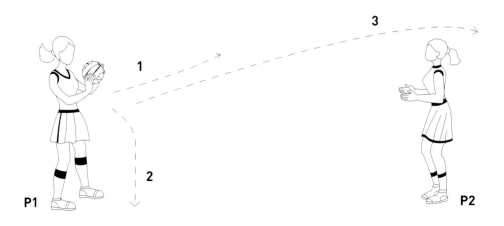

1

2

3

P1

P2

Objective: To practise moving to gather a loose ball and maintaining control and balance ready to make the next pass.

Equipment: One ball between two players.

Description: Player 1, as the feeder, starts with the ball. Player 2, the worker, stands facing P1 approximately 5 m away. P1 will feed the ball into the working space for P2 to move into and collect the ball as quickly as she can, obeying the footwork rule and then returning the ball to P1 before returning to the start point. P1 chooses where to place the ball and calls an instruction for P2 to respond to, i.e. left, right, front, the space about 1–2m in front of her, low, the space immediately in front of her feet etc. P1 should drop the ball into the space as she calls the instruction so the ball rolls on the floor making it more difficult for P2 to retrieve it.

Coaching points: Look for explosive reactions from the worker – the response should be immediate and she should aim to get to the ball and snatch it up before it has bounced too many times or rolled too far – as if a loose ball in a game. Encourage the worker to use short steps as she reaches the ball and control her body to avoid a footwork fault. Encourage her to snatch the ball up and adopt a balanced body position before making the pass back to P1. Build this drill slowly as the worker develops control and confidence, working up to a continuous controlled drill.

drill 32 *get free*

Objective: To practise dodging and footwork skills to get free from a defender, and timing of the pass.

Equipment: One ball, six markers between six players.

Description: Set up an area equivalent to about one third of a court. Divide the players into two teams – attackers have the ball and defenders have to try and intercept it. Players must not pass back to the player from whom they receive the ball. When the ball gets intercepted or a pass is lost, the groups swap roles.

Coaching points: Encourage accuracy of passing and lots of communication. Don't let fatigue lead to a sloppy practice. One minute of intense running is a lot! Use the rest at the changeover of roles to reaffirm objectives.

Progression: Four players per team with two balls means that players need to raise awareness as there will be two active balls at any one time. If you have an exceptional group of players then you can try two balls and three players per team!

drill 33 cones drill

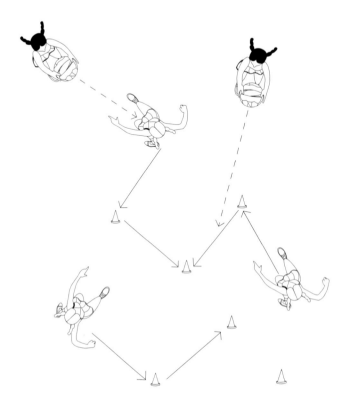

Objective: To develop technique and skills to make quick, controlled changes of direction.

Equipment: Two cones per player (this drill needs at least eight players), and two balls.

Description: Cones are spread randomly over one third of the court. Two players are feeders (F) and stand at the head of the area. The other players run to a cone and push off hard to another, watching the feeders at all times. At will, the feeders pass a ball to a player who receives, lands and returns a pass to the other feeder. (Players may have to pivot to do this.)

Coaching points: Players have to keep their heads up so they don't run into anyone. Limit the length of the drill to 30 seconds and then change the feeders. This means the runners can have a rest every other time. Look for quick and controlled changes of direction, which are achieved by pushing off on the outside foot using the arms and shoulders for balance.

Progression: Introduce more runners.

drill 34 half-moon drill

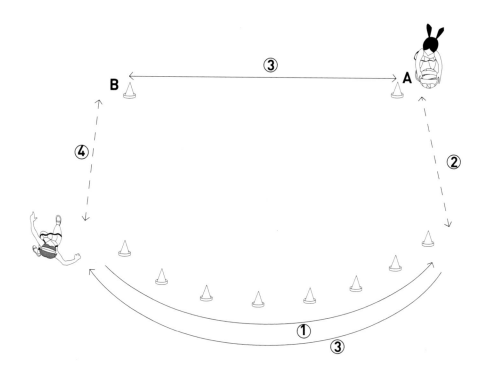

Objective: To develop movement skills and practise passing under pressure.

Equipment: Ten cones and one ball between two players.

Description: Set up eight of the cones in a semicircle. Two more cones are set 2–3 m back at either end of the semicircle. On the coach's command player 1 side steps around the cones. When she gets to the end she lands (two-footed), receives and returns a pass from player 2 (standing at A) and then returns to the other side of the semicircle. By the time they get there, player 2 must have run to B where once again she gives and receives a pass.

Coaching points: This is supposed to be a fast-feet drill so make sure the runner only has a short distance to cover and does not get tired and reduce the quality of her movements. If you use groups of three players, then two can pass and run while the third has one minute to walk slowly around the court to recover.

Progression: Vary the type of passes used.

drill 35 *H drill*

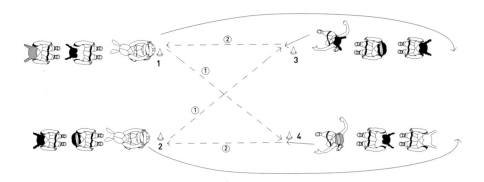

Objective: To practise driving forwards to receive a pass and the timing of a pass.

Equipment: Two balls, four cones.

Description: Using the centre third as the working area, divide the players into four teams and line them up behind the third lines as shown above. Place the cones approximately 1.5 m away from the third lines. The first players behind cones 1 and 2 shoulder pass diagonally into the space ahead of the first players behind cones 3 and 4. The passers then run to the back of the queue opposite them. The receiving players drive onto the pass and make a good landing before giving a straight chest pass to the next player in the queue opposite them, who drives onto the pass. The passers then run to the back of the queue opposite them, and so on.

Coaching points: Walk the drill through once so that everyone knows what they are doing. Encourage a good hard drive onto the passes.

Progression: Change the chest pass to a shoulder or a bounce pass.

drill 36 *ladder passing*

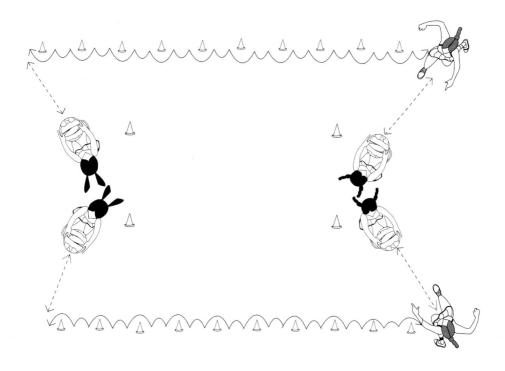

Objective: To develop movement skills and practise passing under pressure.

Equipment: 22 cones and four balls between six players.

Description: Set up two lines of 10 cones 5 m apart, with about 30 cm between cones. Two more cones are set in between the rows at either end (A and B) with two passers back to back at each one. The other two players are the runners, with one standing at the end of each line of cones. On the coach's command the runners side-step over the cones hitting every gap with very fast feet. When they get to the end of the line they land (two-footed) to receive and return a ball from a passer, then return to the other end of the row of cones in the same way where another passer waits. Each runner completes four passes and then rests. They score a point for each perfect pass, where the passer does not have to move to catch the ball.

Coaching points: This is a fast-feet drill so ensure plenty of recovery time.

Progression: Vary the type of passes used.

Renae Hallinan (Australia) looking to pass the ball demonstrating good, balanced shoulder pass technique.

BALL SKILLS –
PASSING AND CATCHING

It is fairly obvious that the ability to give and receive a pass is at the heart of the skills needed to become a good netballer. However, beyond the basics there are several elements within this training topic that can help develop confidence in throwing and catching the ball.

A common issue with younger, inexperienced players is that they consider possession of the ball to be the end in itself, rather than a link in a team chain. Many of the following drills that focus on passing and catching are also designed to give context to a pass – when, where and why we pass as well as how.

It is important to emphasise that the safe arrival of the ball is the responsibility of the passer – the aim of a pass is to transfer the ball to a co-player, not just to unload responsibility for it. It is the responsibility of the receiver to provide space and a target for the passer by indicating where they want to receive the ball by signalling with their hands.

As skills develop and drills require more movement, balance will become more and more important. Therefore, good practice is vital even within the more simple drills – check–receive–pass–move – maintaining control and balance at all times.

Once again there is the issue of when to stop and restart a drill. There is the constant danger of the players becoming embroiled in the fun of the drill (which is good) and losing sight of the skill that they are practising. It lies with the coach to spot when the drill is drifting and at that point he or she should stop the players and re-communicate the skill being practised and the objectives of the drill.

When passing the ball encourage players to:

- Keep fingers well spread behind the ball to help with control.
- Transfer their weight forwards from the back foot to the front to help give power to the pass.
- Look into the space where they are passing the ball and finish the pass by following the ball with their arm(s) and fingers extended in the direction they want the ball to go – this helps to avoid high looping passes that take longer to travel the distance and are more easily intercepted.
- Pass the ball into the space in front of the receiver, ahead of their fingers, not behind them. The catcher might have to reach for the ball, especially if receiving a pass while on the move.

When catching a ball encourage players to:

- Watch the ball into their hands. Players often drop a ball because they are already looking to where the next pass is going to be.

- Stretch arms and fingers out towards the ball to catch it and step forwards to meet the ball rather than waiting for the ball to reach them. Fingers should be spread and 'W' shaped with thumbs behind the ball.
- Catch with two hands and snatch the ball into the body, cushioning the catch with bent elbows.
- Bring two hands onto the ball quickly if a catch is made with one hand to ensure control and balance for the next pass.

Younger players need to learn which type of pass to use when, the control and accuracy of the pass, and understand the concept of throwing the ball into a space to enable the receiver to run onto and catch the ball more easily. This involves strength, balance, quick decision-making and spatial awareness – difficult concepts to master!

Even for players with some experience of netball, revisiting basic passing technique is a benefit and will help ensure good habits, consistency and accuracy. Don't be afraid of going back to basics, although make sure this is balanced with progression to keep everyone interested.

Some players have a tendency to throw high looping lob-type passes which have little control or accuracy. A lob pass is a legitimate pass and requires good technique to be accurate. Don't accept a sloppy version as an alternative during practices – this will help reduce the chance of these passes being used in games.

coaching points

Remember the points above for passing and catching for all passes.

Chest pass: A pass aimed at covering short distances quickly. A good chest pass travels in a straight line from the thrower's chest height to the catcher's chest height – no loopiness!
Technique:

- Both hands behind the ball, fingers making a 'W' shape with the ball held close to the chest and bent elbows relaxed at the sides.
- The fingers and wrist control and direct the pass.

Shoulder pass: A pass aimed at covering a greater distance and requiring a different technique to the chest pass. Thrown from shoulder height, the shoulder pass can be a one- or two-handed pass. This pass can be a direct pass travelling in a straight line from one player to another, or it can be an angled pass looping over the head of a defender. When moving the ball up the court encourage players to make the shoulder pass a strong, straight pass and avoid the looped pass which is easier to intercept and is less accurate.
Technique:

- Stand side on to the person receiving the pass with feet shoulder-width apart, knees slightly bent and the body weight on the back foot. The opposite foot to the throwing arm is forward.

- The ball is held at shoulder height behind the shoulder with the elbow bent, either on one hand or with two hands.
- The ball is pushed forward using the shoulder, elbow, wrist and fingers and involves a twisting movement from the shoulder and waist.

Bounce pass: A specialised pass aimed at covering a shorter distance and avoiding the arms of defenders. The ball takes longer to travel the distance because of the bounce, and accuracy is vital to avoid loss of possession through interceptions. A quick bounce pass into the circle to a shooter is a good way of avoiding good defence. This does require practice for younger players.
   Technique:

- A bounce pass can be made with one or two hands from hip or waist height and from the side or the front of the body.
- The bounce should be approximately $2/3$ of the distance between the person making the pass and the receiver.

Lob pass: A specialised pass aimed at looping the ball high over the head of a defender. This can be used effectively to feed the ball into a shooter who is holding her space under the post. A lob pass can also be used throughout the court and should be selected because it benefits the team and not just as an excuse for a shoulder pass! Timing is crucial to avoid the defender intercepting from a well-timed jump and this also requires practice.
   Technique:

- The pass can be made face on or sideways to the receiver.
- The ball is held in one or two hands above the head with elbows slightly bent.
- The ball is released from above the head using a push from the elbows and directed with the fingers and wrists.
- The ball travels in a high arc motion and the arms move upwards and forwards slightly as the ball leaves the hands finishing high above the head.
- The highest point of the arc of the ball should be when it is over the defender's head making it harder for her to intercept.

Objective: To practise quick reactions and develop hand-eye co-ordination.

Equipment: One ball between two players.

Description: Player 1 starts with the ball and is the feeder. Player 2 is the worker and stands facing P1 approximately 1.5m apart. To start, P1 makes short, sharp chest passes to P2 varying the placement of the pass to the centre, left and right so P2 has to stretch her arm out to catch the ball and snatch it in – her feet should stay still. P2 quickly returns the ball to P1 after each pass. After several passes, P1 places the ball slightly further to the left and right, making P2 take one step to the side in order to reach the ball. After several passes swap roles.

Coaching points: This is a quick drill in a small space to help players practise quick reactions so they need to be ready and on their toes. Look for accurate passes from both players. Encourage P2 to reach out with one hand to gather the ball and quickly bring the other hand to it to snatch it in to her body before returning the pass to P1. There should be very little movement from P2 when she is catching the ball so P1 must be accurate with her passing.

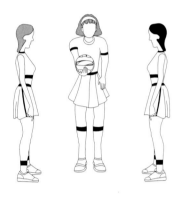

Objective: To introduce and practise the toss-up and improve reaction time.

Equipment: One ball between groups of three.

Description: The toss-up is a means of giving both players an even chance of catching the ball if an infringement on court is judged to be simultaneous by the umpire. Players A and B stand facing each other 1 m apart with their feet shoulder-width apart and hands by their sides. (In a game the players would face the way their team is shooting and all other players would need to be at least 1 m away). The player with the ball (C) stands in between the players close enough to be able to step forwards and hold the ball in the middle of A and B at shoulder height. Player C balances the ball on one hand with the palm facing upwards. She steps forwards to place the ball in between players A and B tossing the ball straight up to about shoulder height of the smallest player and at the same time shouting go. Players A and B both try to snatch the ball. If either player moves before player C shouts 'go' (or the umpire blows the whistle) the ball is given to the other player. The player who cleanly catches the ball gets one point. No points are given if the ball is dropped. After five attempts swap roles.

Coaching points: As it is usually the umpire who takes a toss-up it is useful for players to be able to practise this with the coach responding to a whistle. Look for a balanced position at the start. Players should be ready to move, knees slightly bent with arms by their side. Encourage players to watch the ball as the umpire/coach brings it forward to make the toss-up – this helps with anticipation and quick reaction. Encourage the players to snatch the ball into their body away from their opposing player.

drill 39 *chest pass*

Objective: To develop confidence in good chest pass technique to ensure accuracy and consistency.

Equipment: One ball per pair.

Description: Starting with the players 3 m apart, have the players execute chest passes between each other.

Coaching points: This pass should be flat and firm, from chest height to chest height. Players should keep elbows high and fingers spread wide behind the ball and follow through to the target with the fingertips. Encourage players to reach out to catch the ball early, rather than waiting for the ball to come to them.

Progression: Once correct technique is understood, have the players widen the gap between each other to test where the limits of accuracy are.

drill 40 *shoulder pass*

Objective: To develop confidence in good shoulder pass technique to ensure consistency and accuracy.

Equipment: One ball per pair.

Description: Starting with the players 5 m apart, have the players execute shoulder passes between each other using alternating arms.

Coaching points: Focus on setting good habits in setting up the pass correctly and transferring the body weight in the direction of the pass to add power. Accuracy with a shoulder pass is harder to achieve at the start, with the pass looping between players or not covering the required distance through poor technique or lack of power. Encourage players to practise a one-handed shoulder pass with their dominant hand and a two-handed shoulder pass. Players should step forwards as they make the pass, transferring their weight and twisting their shoulder to follow the ball – the end of the pass should result in their arm and fingers pointing in the direction of the pass, with their head up looking towards the receiver. Looped shoulder passes result from mistiming the release of the ball or the arm movement pointing skywards instead of straight out at shoulder height. Shoulder passes that do not cover the distance lack strength, practising moving the body weight forwards in time with releasing the ball will add power. Keep everything slow and controlled to allow players to get the feel of the pass.

Progression: Once correct technique is understood, have the players widen the gap between each other to test where the limits of accuracy are.

drill 41 *the lob 1*

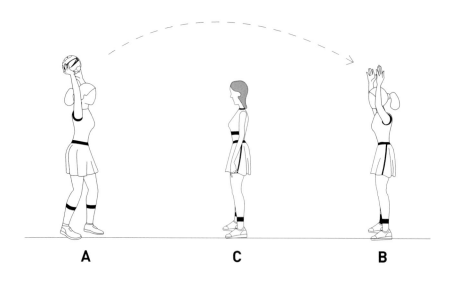

A   C   B

Objective: To develop confidence in good lob pass technique to ensure consistency and accuracy.

Equipment: One ball between groups of three.

Description: Player A stands with the ball facing player B, approximately 3 m apart. Player C is a defender and stands in front of player B facing player A. At this stage the defender should stand still to present a barrier between the thrower and receiver. Player A lobs the ball to player B aiming for good technique and over the head of player C. After five attempts swap roles.

Coaching points: Look for a controlled pass that loops over the head of the defender with the highest point of the arc being when the ball is directly over the head of the defender. Encourage the receiver to be ready to catch the ball with arms raised. Remember, young players tend to default to a lob-type pass when under pressure – don't accept sloppy technique, instead instil good habits. This is an effective pass that can be used to feed a ball over a defender – it can also be easy to read and intercept for a determined, athletic defender!

Progression: As confidence and accuracy improves encourage the receiver to jump to catch the ball in the air.

drill 42 the lob 2

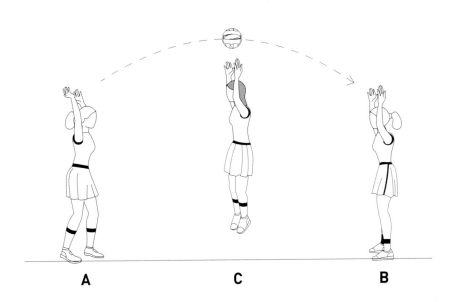

A   C   B

Objective: To continue to develop confidence in good lob pass technique to ensure consistency and accuracy.

Equipment: One ball between groups of three.

Description: This is a progression from drill 41 introducing an active defender which requires more accuracy from the thrower. Player A stands with the ball facing player B, approximately 3 m apart. Player C is a defender and stands in front of player B facing player A and should try to intercept the pass by jumping to catch the ball. Player A lobs the ball to player B aiming for good technique and over the head of player C. After five attempts swap roles.

Coaching points: Look for a controlled pass that loops over the head of the defender with the highest point of the arc being when the ball is directly over the head of the defender. Encourage the receiver and the defender to be ready to catch/intercept the ball with arms raised and jump to try and snatch the ball out of the air. Watch out for contact from either player as they jump to catch the ball.

Progression: Introduce a second defender to try and mark player A as they throw the lob, facing player A with arms up. Watch for the correct distance from the new defender.

drill 43 bounce pass

Objective: To practise the bounce pass.

Equipment: One ball per team.

Description: Divide the group into teams of eight. Set up the teams in a zigzag formation, with approximately 2 m between teams. On the coach's command, the ball is passed up the line using a bounce pass.

Coaching points: Younger players will get excited as they become engrossed in the drill and will want to unload the ball quickly instead of executing a good pass. If this becomes a problem, tell the players that they are responsible for the ball until the receiver has caught it, so if a pass is dropped or missed then the passer has to retrieve it and run back to make a new pass.

Progression: This drill can be made continuous by asking the players to run to the end of the line after they have passed. If you have two teams, an element of competition can be introduced by setting a distance to be covered by the team.

drill 44 *turn and catch*

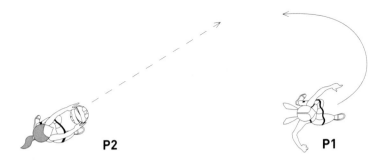

P2   P1

Objective: To develop quick reactions and catching skills and introduce the idea of turning the body to receive a pass.

Equipment: One ball between two players.

Description: Set up the players approximately 2m apart. Player 2 starts with the ball. Player 1 is working and stands with her back to player 2. Player 2 shouts 'left' or 'right' and player 1 must turn quickly in that direction to receive a pass. Player 2 should only pass the ball once player 1 has turned and is facing her. After five goes, swap roles.

Coaching points: Look for a quick reaction and a controlled turn by player 1. Passes should be accurate and timed to only be released when the player is ready.

Progression: Vary the type of pass. Increase the distance between players. When players are turning and receiving the ball confidently, the feeder can pass the ball into the space for the other player to move onto. Add a defender to face the feeder to try to make an interception. This makes the timing and placing of the pass more critical to avoid the defender.

drill 45 *triangles*

Objective: To develop quick, accurate passing and improve reaction time.

Equipment: Two balls between three players.

Description: Players A, B and C stand in a triangle sufficiently far apart to allow a chest pass between each player. Players B and C each have a ball. Player B throws the ball to player A who returns it. Player C then passes the ball to player A who returns it. This is repeated, seeing how fast the ball can be fed and received without anyone dropping it.

Coaching points: Quick, accurate passing and bags of concentration are essential.

Progression: Increase the distance between the players and change the type of pass to a shoulder pass or bounce pass, for example.

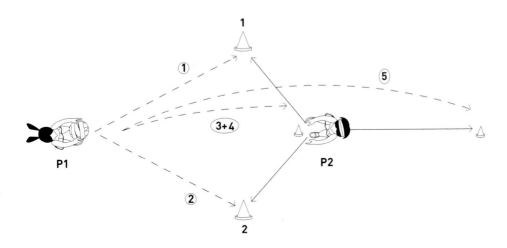

Objective: To develop confidence in timing the pass and controlling momentum to make an accurate pass.

Equipment: One ball between two, two cones.

Description: P1, the feeder, starts with the ball. P2, the worker, stands facing P1 approximately 5 m away. Place the cones as shown, approximately 3 m out to the side halfway between P1 and P2. P2 sprints diagonally towards cone 1 to receive a chest pass from P2 as she reaches the cone. P2 lands two footed, makes a quick return chest pass to P1 and sidesteps back to the start point to immediately sprint to cone 2 and repeat the landing/ passing sequence. As P2 returns to the start point from the second pass P1 makes a shoulder pass for P2 to jump, land and catch at the start. P2 returns the ball to P1 using a shoulder pass and immediately moves backwards to receive an overhead pass which she catches, lands and returns to P1 using a shoulder pass. Repeat three times and swap roles.

Coaching points: This drill needs space to allow quick movement, landing and shoulder passes. Look for explosive forward speed from the working player, driving diagonally forwards to receive the pass at the cone. Stress the importance of controlled movement and a balanced and controlled landing before they return the pass to the feeder. When receiving the overhead pass the worker should make small backwards steps, feet shoulder-width apart facing the feeder, and time her jump to catch the ball in the air. The feeder needs to time her pass so the ball reaches the space the working player is moving into at the correct moment. Passes from both players should be accurate. Build this drill slowly to work up to a fast-paced continuous drill with accurate passing and controlled footwork.

drill 47 catch-up squares

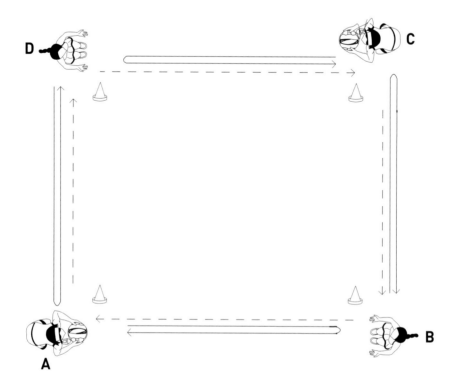

Objective: To improve passing and movement skills.

Equipment: Two balls and four cones.

Description: Set up a square with the cones about 3 m apart. The balls are diagonally opposite each other at the start. Players A and C roll a ball along the side of the square to the player at the 'free' corner (B and D). Players A and C then follow the ball by running to the next corner and back to receive the next 'pass'. A pass cannot be given until the receiver is back on station at their original corner. The objective is to catch up with the other ball or to last one minute – whichever comes first.

Coaching points: This drill will break down as soon as one ball catches up. At this point stop the drill and re-start from the beginning. Ensure that everyone concentrates on giving a good pass and not just 'unloading' in panic and appreciates that a ball travels faster than a runner – a good lesson in itself!

Progression: When the rolled ball version of this drill is mastered then move on to a bounce pass, chest pass and so on.

drill 48 *passing square*

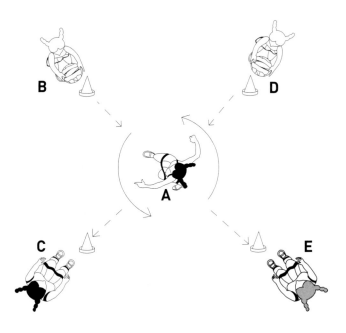

Objective: To practise passing and receiving the ball while changing direction by pivoting.

Equipment: Two balls and four cones between five players.

Description: Use the cones to mark out a square with sides of 3–4 metres, depending on the passing ability of the players. The distance between the cones should be large enough for the pass, but shouldn't place too much pressure on the players. Player A stands in the middle of the square with the other four players standing on the corners. Players B and D each have a ball. Player B feeds the ball to player A, who catches the ball and passes it to player E. Player A pivots to receive a pass from player D and passes the ball on to player C, and so on.

Coaching points: Ensure that one foot remains stationary while passing. Start the drill very slowly and only increase the pace once everyone has grasped it.

Progression: Vary the type of pass used and speed up the feed of the pass.

drill 49 *circle game*

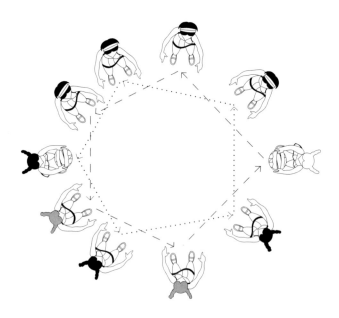

Objective: To practise catching and receiving passes while introducing an element of competition.

Equipment: Two teams with a minimum of four players in each, two balls.

Description: Two teams (A and B) stand in a large circle, each team taking alternate places. Players should stand at least one arm's width apart. Start with the balls on opposite sides of the circle, one with team A and one with team B. On the coach's whistle the ball is passed around the circle between members of the same team, i.e. players from team A pass their ball to each other only and players from team B pass the ball to each other only. The balls are passed in the same direction and the aim is to try and overtake the other team's ball.

Coaching points: The players will have to pivot to receive and give a pass.

Progression: As above, introducing a change of direction on the coach's whistle. Attempts at intercepting the opposite team's ball can also be introduced.

drill 50 pea on a drum

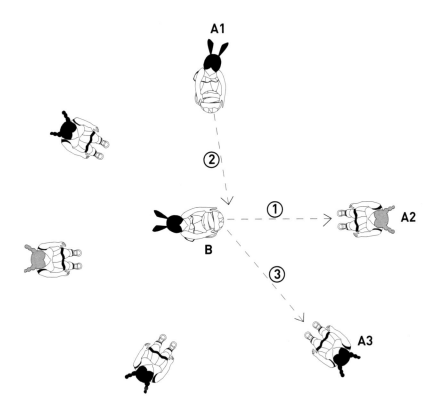

Objective: To practise passing under pressure.

Equipment: Two balls between at least seven players.

Description: Arrange six players (A1–A6) into a circle with the remaining player (B) in the centre with a ball. Another ball is given to A1. B passes the ball to A2. A1 then passes the ball to B who immediately passes to A3. The moment the pass is away A2 passes to B and so on. There is therefore a continuous stream of passes coming to B, who must receive and give quickly and accurately. Change player B regularly.

Coaching points: Don't sacrifice quality for speed. If the drill breaks down, return to slow, careful passing and then slowly build back up.

Progression: By increasing the spacing between the circle players, B will have to pivot to make the pass. Watch for footwork if you progress to this level. If you have a group that is really good at this (and perhaps getting a bit cocky) then call for changes of direction and type of pass.

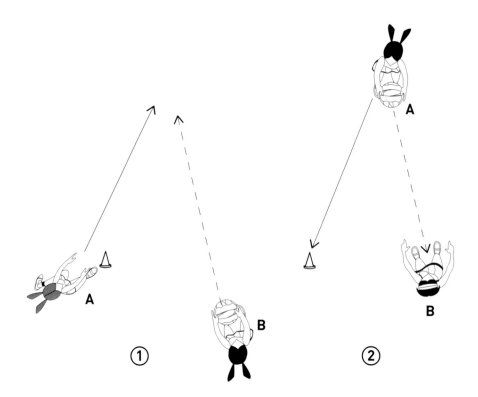

Objective: To develop spatial awareness and improve passing into space.

Equipment: One ball and one cone between two players.

Description: Partners stand facing each other approximately 2 m apart. A stands at the cone and on the coach's command runs diagonally to the right of player B, who passes the ball in front of the running player. A catches the ball, pivots and returns the ball to B. A returns to the cone. On the next command, A runs to the left and the pass into space is repeated. After five passes to each side, partners exchange roles. Repeat so each person runs and throws twice, then allow recovery. Discuss what has just happened and reaffirm drill objectives before re-starting.

Coaching points: Passes must be in front of the running player to ensure they run onto the ball and don't have to reach backwards or stop to catch the pass.

Progression: B calls 'left', 'right', 'front' or 'back' and A must respond by running in that direction to receive the pass.

drill 52 *flag drill*

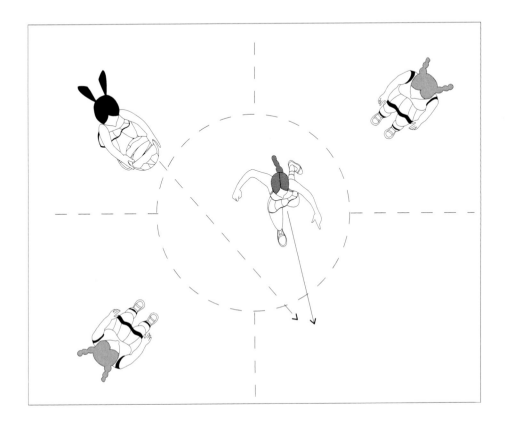

Objective: To practise using and creating space.

Equipment: Centre third of the court divided into five spaces, four players, one ball.

Description: The four players take up position as shown above, one per sector (there will always be one empty space). Player 1 has the ball. On the coach's command, player 1 passes to a player of her choice. Meanwhile the player closest to the empty space drives into it and calls for a pass. Players are asked to be aware of where the space is now and where it is going to be next.

Coaching points: Start off slowly so players can get a feel of the drill and only then speed things up. Never sacrifice quality for speed.

Progression: Build the drill by gradually adding one, two, three and then four defenders to the grid.

drill 53 diamonds

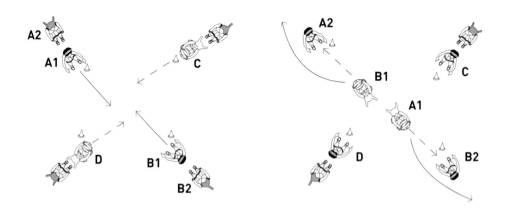

Objective: To improve movement skills, spatial awareness, communication and conditioning.

Equipment: Two balls and four cones between eight players.

Description: Place cones to form a square approximately five metres across. Two players stand at each cone. Players A and B are diagonally opposite each other, with players C and D at the other two cones with a ball. A and B run towards each other, and when they reach the middle of the square they each receive a pass from their left from C and D respectively. A passes forwards to the next player (B2) and B passes to player A2. A and B then run and stand behind the player to whom they passed the ball. C and D then run, receive the pass from A2 and B2 and so on.

Coaching points: Players should always receive the ball from the left and throw straight ahead. Walk through the drill a few times then build up speed gradually.

Progression: Perform the same drill but players receive passes from the right.

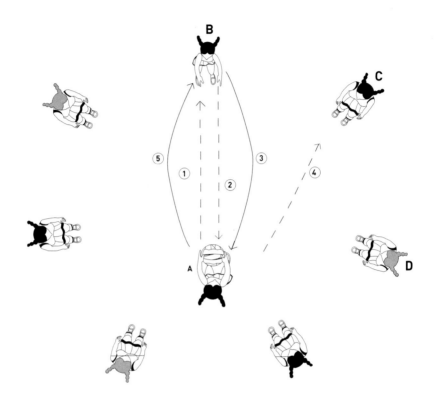

Objective: To practise passing and moving into a space.

Equipment: One ball, a chalked circle 5 m in diameter.

Description: Player A stands in the middle of the circle holding the ball. She throws the ball to player B, who returns the pass to player A and follows the ball to the centre of the circle. Player A throws the ball to player C and moves out of the centre to the space in the circle left by player B. Player C passes the ball to player B in the centre, following the ball. Player B passes the ball to player D and moves into the space left by Player C, and so on.

Coaching points: Communication is vital – you can never have too much! The next receiver needs to be the eyes of the passer, who will have enough on her plate trying to avoid running players, catching and so on. The receiver needs to be in a position to take an easy pass.

Progression: The speed and type of pass can be varied. The player moving out of the centre can defend the ball as she moves out to the circle edge.

drill 55 *box drill*

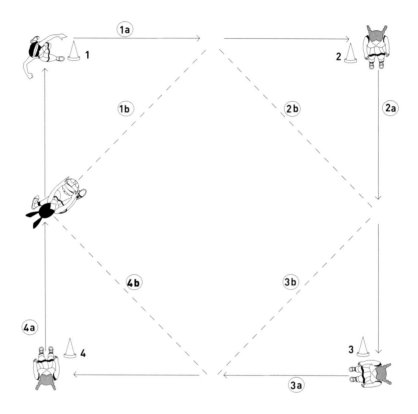

Objective: To practise receiving a pass from an angle.

Equipment: Four cones and one ball between five players.

Description: Place the cones in a 10 m square. Four players stand at a cone, player 1 at cone 1 and so on. The remaining player stands between cone 4 and cone 1 with the ball. On the coach's command player 1 runs towards cone 2 to receive a pass from player 5 halfway between the cones. Player 5 then runs to cone 1 to take up the space vacated by player 1. As soon as player 1 receives the ball, player 2 runs towards cone 3 and player 1 delivers a pass to be received halfway between cones 2 and 3, and runs on to cone 2, and so on.

Coaching points: Ensure players drive out hard for each pass. The pass should be into space and not at a receiver. This is a complex drill that should be walked through initially, so that everyone can then concentrate on passing, landing and pushing off.

Progression: Vary the types of pass. Change the direction of rotation.

drill 56 *ball tag*

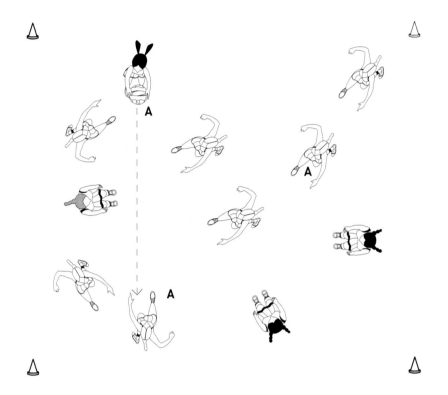

Objective: To develop communication and passing skills.

Equipment: One ball, four cones.

Description: Use the cones to mark out an area equivalent to approximately one third of the court. There are three attackers (A) and lots of evaders. The aim is for the attackers to tag the evaders with the ball. Once tagged the evader must stand still. The attackers cannot run if they are in possession of the ball but can pivot on one foot.

Coaching points: Encourage lots of communication and movement between attackers. Look for quick but accurate passing.

Progression: Change the attackers regularly and see how many evaders they can tag in a fixed amount of time, for example two minutes.

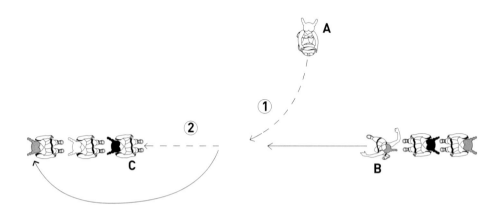

Objective: To practise running into a space to receive an accurate pass.

Equipment: One ball per group.

Description: Players form two lines facing each other approximately 8 m apart with player A, the feeder, standing with the ball halfway between the two teams. Player B runs towards the opposite team to receive a pass from player A. Player B catches the ball and then throws it to player C at the front of the opposite team. Player B then runs to the back of this line. Player C returns the ball to player A, then makes her run towards the opposite team to receive the next pass from player A, and so on.

Coaching points: Look for accurate passing with the ball passed into space in front of the receiving player. Players sprint to receive the ball, jumping with a balanced landing to avoid stepping before making a pass.

Progression: Rather than landing, stopping and passing, the ball should be released straight away. This running pass should still be balanced and accurate.

drill 58 timing

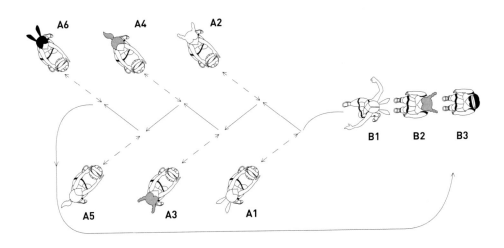

Objective: To develop confidence in timing the pass and passing into the space for a player to move in to catch the ball.

Equipment: At least eight players each with a ball between two, and cones.

Description: Each passer (A) has a ball and is positioned in a long, staggered grid as shown above. There should be sufficient space between each player to allow B players to run into the space to receive the pass. The receivers (B) form a line starting 5 m from the start of the grid area. B1 sprints into the grid towards A1 who passes the ball to B1 aiming for it to be received at X. B1 lands two-footed, catches the ball and returns the pass to A1. B1 then pushes off with her left foot to turn and sprint towards A2 to receive a pass as before. B1 continues through the grid and walks to return to the end of the B line and recover. B2 starts the drill when there is sufficient space to do so – and so on.

Coaching points: This drill needs space! Look for strong sprinting to drive into the space to receive the pass and a determined push off the outside foot to help with change of direction. Stress the importance of a balanced and controlled landing. The feeders need to time the pass to reach the space B is moving into in time for her to catch the ball cleanly – the pass should not be behind her or too early. Build the drill slowly – it is designed to build confidence in receiving a strong pass moving into a space.

Sara Bayman of England is blocked from passing the ball by Australia's Natalie von Bertouch.

ATTACKING AND DEFENDING

Although there are specific attacking and defending positions in a netball team all players need to be able to adopt both an attacking and a defending role within a game, depending on the situation. The change between the two can happen very quickly and to be successful, players will need to be able to anticipate and recognise these changes in order to quickly respond and react appropriately.

This is easier for some players than others; some are naturally able to 'read' the game and anticipate what will happen next. This enables them to adopt the role necessary, move into the spaces quickly or block an opponent's move effectively. For others, this does not come naturally and they require lots of practice to understand the game and the changing situations. Encouraging players to recognise when their team is attacking and defending is a good start!

Within this section many of the skills developed previously will be put into a game context. Court and spatial awareness are now added to passing and movement skills. Attacking and defending have been paired together as the majority of the drills that practise one also provide an opportunity to practise the other. In addition, there is also the opportunity to develop 'controlled aggression'; the desire to win the ball and the determination to gain possession and never give up – qualities that all good netballers possess.

When players become more experienced and are better able to anticipate the flow of the game and utilise the space available, more advanced defensive skills, zoning and blocking techniques, can be introduced.

key coaching points

1   Defenders need to have controlled, balanced footwork to be able to move quickly in all directions. They also need to be able to jump! It is surprising how many players seem to have their feet rooted to the ground – especially if they are tall. Encourage all players to jump up to meet the ball whatever their size.
2   Defenders need to keep going and remain calm under pressure, even when it appears their efforts are wasted. Younger players can panic in pressured situations and a calm coach can help them keep going! Perseverance is key; try to ensure players understand that their efforts are having a positive impact on the game by putting the attack off or forcing mistakes, and encourage them to keep going.
3   Encourage all defending players to mark the ball with both arms up and outstretched – the aim being to make it as difficult for the attacker to pass the ball as possible. Remember they need to be 1 m away from the player with the ball.
4   The ultimate aim of attackers is to score goals! Developing confidence and experience will help them work together as a team, improve their awareness of space, each other and the passes they can use.

5 When attacking, i.e. in possession of the ball, encourage players to move towards the person with the ball and not run away or stand still! Moving towards the ball helps make the next pass easier. Players obviously have to work with the space and know to make a second or third move into a space for a pass if the first attempt is not successful. Watch out for young, inexperienced players all running around the player with the ball like bees to a honey pot; encourage more thoughtful movement and space awareness around the court and remember this is a hard concept for some young players and takes time to sink in!

golden rule

All players should be determined to get the ball and never give up chasing – it is surprising how many loose balls on court are reached or how many balls are prevented from going out of court by the dogged, enthusiastic player who chases every ball and never gives up!

As my netball teacher used to say, 'The netball court is the only place I want to see you snatching the ball!' A good habit to get into.

drill 59 *cut the cake*

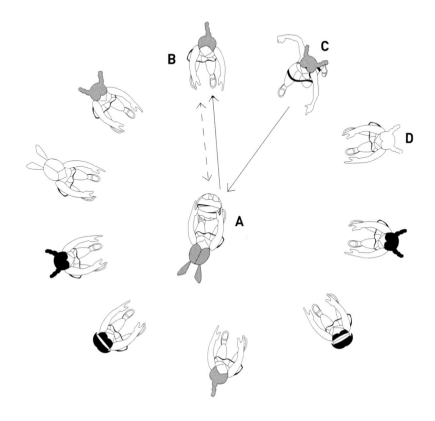

Objective: To practise marking the ball.

Equipment: One ball between 11 players.

Description: Form a circle with one player in the middle. A is in the centre of the circle and has the ball. A passes to one of the players in the circle (B), then runs to defend B's pass. The player next to B, player C, runs into the middle of the circle and receives a pass from B, which A tries to intercept. C then passes the ball to the next player in the circle (D) and runs to defend. Repeat until all the players have been in the middle.

Coaching points: Watch spacing with the defenders. Encourage lots of energy, movement and communication. Insist on good-quality passes at all times.

drill 60 my ball!

Objective: To practise competing in the air for the ball to make an interception.

Equipment: One ball between groups of three.

Description: One player starts with the ball and stands approximately 3 m away from the other two players who stand side by side with their shoulders just touching. The feeder throws the ball to the players, alternating between low and high passes. The players compete to see who can retrieve the ball first.

Coaching points: This is a competitive drill – watch out for barging! Encourage players to be 'ready' – on the balls of their feet, knees slightly bent, watching the ball waiting to react.

Start ⟶

Objective: To practise jumping to tip the ball in the air.

Equipment: One ball between two players.

Description: Divide the players into pairs. Player 1 is working. Player 2 stands balancing the ball high above her head in one hand. Player 1 takes a short run-up and jumps high, aiming to tip the ball off the hand of her partner. She should aim to tip the ball and not knock the arm or hand of the other player, which would be contact in a game situation. If the ball is tipped, player 1 should try to catch it, or retrieve it quickly. Swap roles after five attempts.

Coaching points: It is useful to pair players of similar heights to make this drill even. Look for a controlled run-up and a correctly timed jump to tip the ball only. Encourage player 1 to chase the tipped ball and catch it if possible.

Progression: If the ball is tipped, both players should try to retrieve the ball – watch out for contact!

drill 62 *shadows*

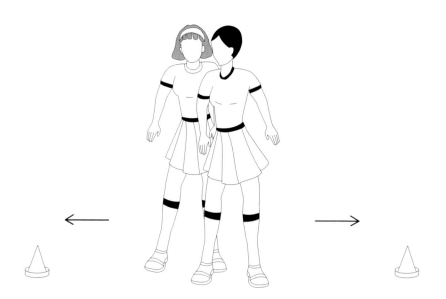

Objective: To practise marking another player.

Equipment: Two players.

Description: Players 1 and 2 stand next to each other. Player 1 moves around the court using different steps and directions i.e. side step, backwards, forwards and so on, moving quickly and slowly. Player 2 has to stay as close to her partner as possible. Change over when the whistle blows.

Coaching points: The aim is to keep as close to your partner as possible, like a shadow, following her movements.

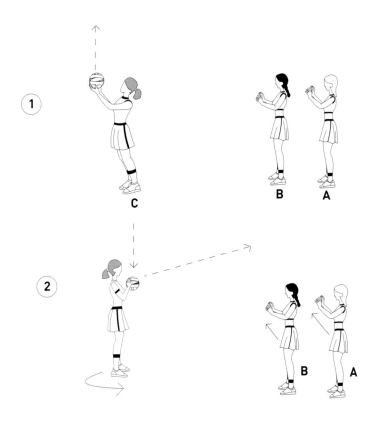

Objective: To practice quick reactions and movement to try to intercept the pass.

Equipment: One ball between three players.

Description: Player A stands behind player B, the defender. Player C stands with her back to the other players, holding the ball. Player C throws the ball in the air, catches it and pivots to throw to player A. Player A indicates which way she is going to move: left, right or overhead. Player C must throw the ball without hesitating and player B tries to intercept the pass.

Coaching points: Attackers should use hand as well as verbal signals to indicate direction of feed. Player C can try using eye-feints to try to throw off the defender. The defender should stand slightly sideways on to the attacker so that she can keep one eye on both players instead of 'ball watching'. Look for players on their toes, attentive and ready to receive or intercept the pass.

Progression: Vary the type of pass. Introduce a second defensive player to defend the pass made by player C.

drill 64 *interceptor 2*

Objective: To practise timing when intercepting a ball.

Equipment: One ball between three players.

Description: Players 2 and 3 stand facing each other 3 m apart, chest passing to each other. Player 1 stands behind player 2 and tries to intercept the pass, timing her run around player 2 to avoid contact and reach the ball first.

Coaching points: All players should be on their toes and be ready to move. Player 1 must time her move to intercept the pass.

Progressions: Vary the type of pass. Lengthen the distance of the pass. The interceptor can move to intercept the ball by jumping around the shoulders of the static catcher, landing to catch the ball. At its most advanced, this practice can be set up for the working player to intercept consecutive passes between the feeders. The distance between the feeders should be kept to 3 m for this to work well.

drill 65 rollerball

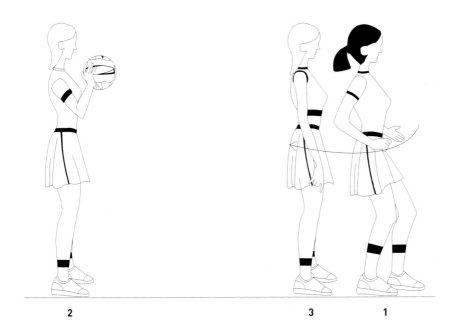

2   3   1

Objective: To introduce the concept of a rolling movement as a form of evasion.

Equipment: One ball between groups of three.

Description: Player 1 is the worker, player 2 the feeder and player 3 the defender. P1 stands 3–4 m away from P2 who has the ball, facing the opposite way. P2 calls 'Go' and P1 'rolls' off to the right to receive a pass – she must quickly try to make eye contact with P2 who releases the ball when eye contact is made. P1 receives the pass, performs a controlled landing and then returns the ball to P2. P3 stands still as if blocking P1 and providing the barrier for P1 to roll around. P1 returns to the start and the drill is repeated to the opposite side. Swap roles.

Coaching points: Look for the working player pushing off on the correct foot, rolling around the defender and quickly making eye contact with P2 to receive the pass. The move is a roll rather than a sideways shuffle! P2 should pass the ball to be received on the side away from the defender. When the defender is introduced (see Progression) the accuracy and timing of the pass is even more important – encourage P1 to reach out away from the defender to catch the ball. Watch out for contact from the defender – any interceptions or tips need to be made without causing contact.

Progression: Vary the type of pass, make passes low and high. Allow the defender to move to try to intercept or block the move.

drill 66 *dodge and mark*

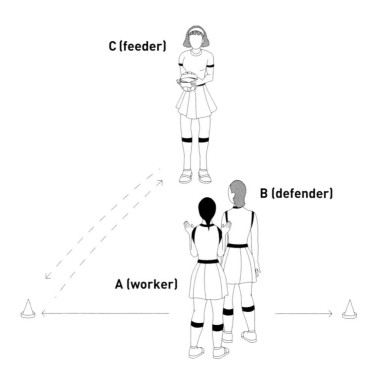

C (feeder)

B (defender)

A (worker)

Objective: To practise dodging to get free from a defender and to practise marking.

Equipment: One ball between three players.

Description: Player A stands behind player B, the defender. Player C stands with the ball facing the other players. Player A must dodge to get free and receive a pass from player C. Player B must try to stick with player A to prevent her receiving the ball.

Coaching points: Look for player A making a definite dodge and indicating where she wants to receive the pass. Eventually, this movement should involve a quick change in direction by pushing off on one foot and using the shoulders to keep the weight moving in the direction in which the player wants to go. Check the position of the defender, who should be marking her player while facing the ball, standing slightly sideways. Her movements should be quick, small side steps to keep up with the attacker. Player C must be ready to pass the ball to player A as soon as she is free.

Progression: Vary the type of pass.

drill 67 *piggies in the middle*

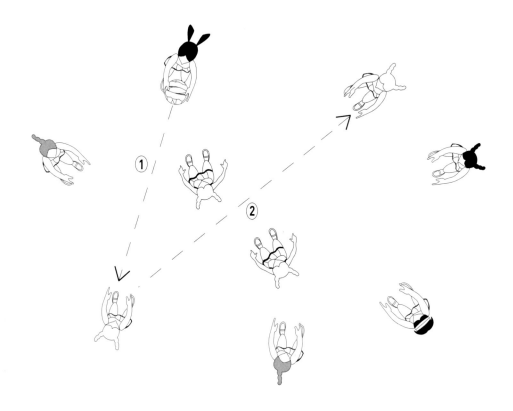

Objective: To practise passing and defensive skills.

Equipment: One ball between nine players.

Description: Form the group into a circle with two players in the centre. The ball is moved across the circle at varying speeds and heights using various types of passes. The players in the middle of the circle try to intercept the ball. Change players after a certain number of passes (start with 20). The 'piggies' keep score of how many touches (one point), knock-downs (three points) or catches (10 points) they make.

Coaching points: Passers must call the name of the person to whom they are passing. Look for quick, accurate passing.

Progression: Try asking the passers to communicate without speaking. Receivers have to signal for the ball (left, right, up, down and so on). Passers can experiment with eye-feints – look at one player and pass to another (very common in basketball but not so common in netball).

drill 68 *marking relay*

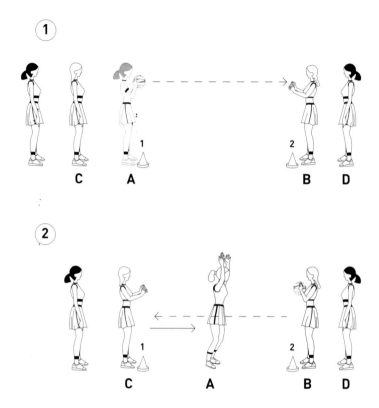

Objective: To practise quick passing and moving to defend the ball.

Equipment: Two cones and one ball.

Description: Split the players into two groups, who line up facing each other approximately 5 m apart behind two cones. Player A starts with the ball and passes ahead to player B. Player A runs to follow the pass and then defends the return pass between players B and C. Once the second pass is made, player A runs to the back of the line. Continue until all players have had three runs each, then stop the drill and reaffirm the objectives and key skills before re-starting.

Coaching points: The players can move between the cones but cannot advance beyond them. Discourage lobbed passes but have the players think about different types of passes (bounce passes to beat a tall player and so on).

drill 69 *triangle drill*

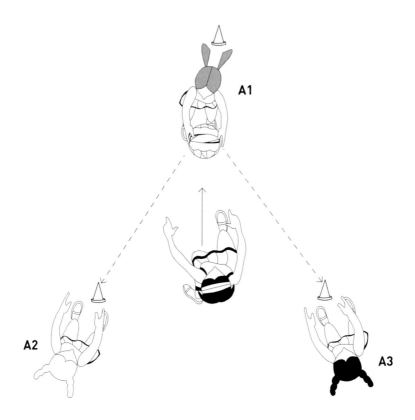

A1

A2

A3

Objective: To practise reading the pass and making an interception.

Equipment: One ball and three cones between four players.

Description: Use the cones to mark out a triangle with sides of approximately 4 m. One player stands on each point of the triangle – these are the attackers, or As. A1 has the ball. The fourth player stands opposite the ball, defending A1's pass to A2 and A3. The defender keeps score of how many touches (one point), knock-downs (three points) or catches (10 points) they make. Rotate the players so there is a new defender and a new passer. Player A can fake the pass to try to fool the defender.

Coaching points: Ensure good fast chest passes or bounce passes, not overhead passes. Encourage the defender to think and talk about what they are watching – the ball or the passer's eyes? They should always react to the ball, not the eyes.

Progression: Adjust the distances between the attackers according to skill and size of the defender to ensure she has a realistic chance of intercepting the ball.

drill 70 *defend the shot*

Objective: To introduce the basic skills of marking a shot for GK and GD.

Equipment: One post, one ball between four players.

Description: GS and GA take it in turns to practise shooting. GK marks GS and GD marks GA to start. In the circle the defender faces the shooting player and tries to make it as difficult for her to make a clean shot as possible by marking the ball with arms outstretched. When the shot has been made all players try to catch any rebound. The ball is passed to the other shooting player and the drill is repeated.

Coaching points: Look for the correct distance from the defending players when marking the shooter to avoid a penalty pass being awarded. Defenders should mark the ball at full stretch, making themselves as tall as possible. Encourage the defender to time their move for the rebound as the shot leaves the shooter's hands, and jump to catch the ball. Make sure the defender does not intimidate the shooter by waving her arms in front of her face or shortening the distance between them.

Progression: As players develop their balance and control encourage the defenders to increase their stretch over the ball by standing on one foot and leaning up and over the ball. This is not suitable for younger players who will find it hard to control their balance.

drill 71 *blocking drill*

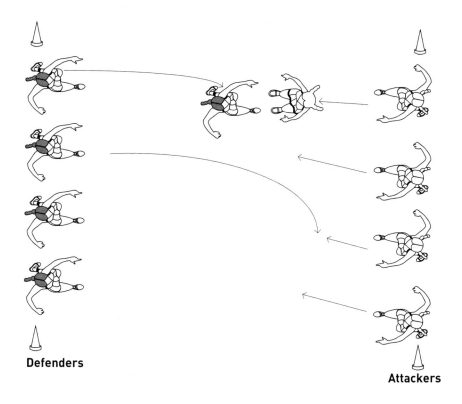

Defenders

Attackers

Objective: To introduce techniques for blocking a moving player.

Equipment: Four cones.

Description: Use the cones to mark out a reasonably large area, maximum size two thirds of the court. Split the players into two groups. One group are the attackers (As) and the second group are the defenders (Ds). Ds line up behind one baseline and As line up on the other baseline, opposite their D partner. The coach gives all As a number and then calls out two numbers at a time. Those two As run and try to get 'home' behind the defenders' baseline. The D partners try and block them out of the area for as long as possible. The Ds can work together and do not have to only block their partner.

Coaching points: Watch for contact at all times and encourage communication. The presence of more than one attacker at a time provides an authentic game environment, but beware of too many players in too small a space.

Progression: Start with one-on-one sessions, then introduce the second pair.

drill 72 *zoning drill*

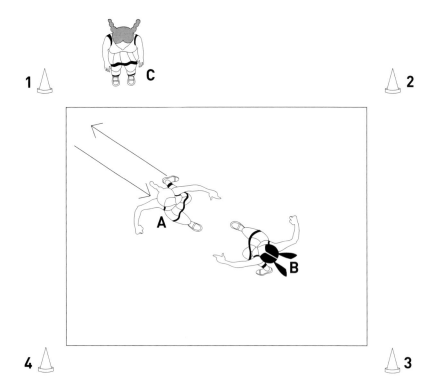

1

2

C

A

B

4

3

Objective: To develop zone marking and blocking skills.

Equipment: Four cones between three players.

Description: Set up the cones to form a square with 5 m sides. Number the cones 1–4. Player A is an attacker, player B is a defender and player C rests. Players A and B start in the centre of the square face to face, on their toes ready to move. Player C calls out a number and player A must try to get to that cone before player B. Player B tries to zone or block her out without contacting her. After three attempts, rotate positions.

Coaching points: Focus on the ready position – not flat-footed, but ready to go! Ensure that player C knows the rules on contact and acts as umpire during the drill.

Progression: Player C has a ball and player A calls the cone number. Player C has to pass towards the designated cone for player A to receive.

drill 73 *ladder drill*

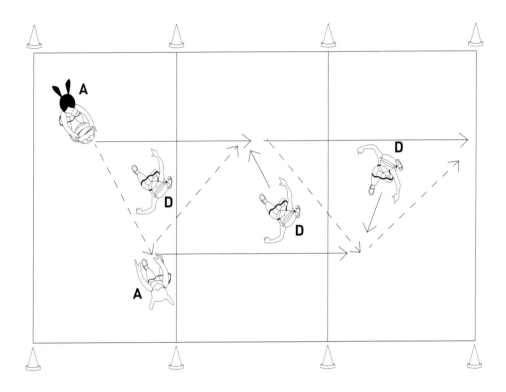

Objective: To improve accurate passing to avoid a defender and practise marking a player.

Equipment: Eight cones and a ball.

Description: Use the cones to set up a grid divided into thirds, each about 5 m by 2.5 m. There should be three defenders and at least two attackers, with one defender per third. The attackers pass the ball to each other along the grid. Each attacker must receive one pass each within each third. The defenders have to try to intercept the ball. If you have extra players, have an extra attacking pair enter the first third once the first pair is clear of it – in this way the drill can be continuous.

Coaching points: Encourage the players to pass the ball into space and create movement in small areas.

Progression: Move the drill into a bigger area and add an extra defender.

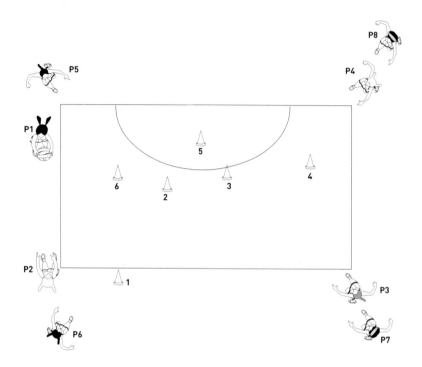

drill 74 give and go drill

Objective: To develop passing skills and driving into a space to receive the ball.

Equipment: One ball, six cones, at least six players.

Description: Set out the area in the goal third as shown. This is a continuous drill involving players passing and moving throughout the area in the following order:

- P1 passes the ball to P2 and then makes a driving run (DR) to cone 1.
- P2 makes a chest pass to P1 at cone 1 and then makes a DR to cone 2 to receive a shoulder pass (SP) from P1.
- P1 runs to corner 2 behind P6.
- P3 makes a DR to cone 3 to receive a CP from P2. P2 runs to the corner 3.
- P4 drives in towards the post and changes direction to receive a quick pass at cone 4 from P3. P3 runs to corner 4.
- P5 drives to cone 6 to receive a shoulder pass across the top of the circle from P4. P4 runs to corner 1.

Coaching points: This is an advanced drill and should be used for more experienced players. Walk the drill through first. Look for players driving forwards into the space, indicating where they are going and making a controlled landing. Timing and accuracy of passing is important.

drill 75 *big pig*

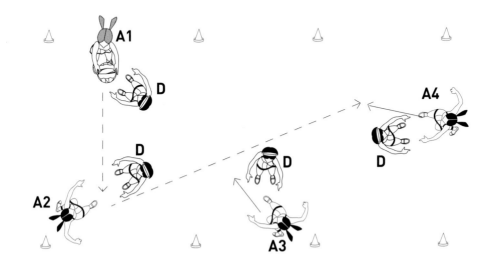

Objective: To develop spatial awareness, and practise passing and marking.

Equipment: One ball, one third of the court, bibs and cones.

Description: Divide the players into two teams, with one team wearing the bibs. One team tries to complete six consecutive passes. The defending team tries to gain possession. Possession also changes with a dropped ball and any infringements set by the coach, for example the ball going out of bounds, footwork and excessively short passes. Passes cannot be returned to the same player.

Coaching points: Defending players can experiment with different types of marking and can also try laying off attackers to try and draw a pass, which they can then try to intercept. The key element is to pass into a space to which a player is moving, not to where they are currently standing.

Progression: Reduced space increases the pressure on the attackers. The drill can be developed by asking the attackers to progress from one side of the court to the other with the defenders trying to stop them. Change the type of pass.

Joanne Harten (England) showing concentration and focus with good shooting technique – essential for successful shooters.

SHOOTING

Shooting is a very specific skill requiring accuracy, good balance, controlled movements and confidence in the shooting circle. Most young players want to be Goal Shooter (GS) or Goal Attack (GA) but often are complacent in these positions, not fully understanding the complexity of the skills required to be a successful shooter.

A GS and GA need to have a good awareness of space within the circle, as well as the ability to take control of that space and maintain focus on a consistent shooting action while under pressure from the defence. Never under estimate the value of shooting practice!

In all the shooting drills to follow there are some key coaching points to consider and skills to encourage. For example:

- Shooters only have 3 seconds to turn and shoot, so the first thing to be sure of is correct balance. Without this, success will be limited. Feet should be shoulder width apart and toes should be pointing towards the net before attempting to make a shot.
- The power and energy for the shot comes from the ground so knees should be bent as if about to jump into the air. The back should be straight with the head up.
- The ball should be held on the fingertips above the head, supported by the other hand – not out in front of the player. The grip should be light, just enough to propel the ball into the net.
- Shooters should try to focus on a point at the back rather than the front of the ring, aiming high for the back of the net. Even if the shot is short, it could still fall in!
- Shooters should aim right before taking the shot and bend their elbows and knees when ready to shoot.
- The ball should be released at the same time as the shooter straightens her legs, moving the arms as little as possible but using a flick of the wrist to add backspin.
- As the shooter prepares to release the ball, she should drop her hands back behind her head. This is the most accurate way to control the direction of the ball.
- The shot should end with the shooter standing on tiptoes with the arms following through towards the ring.

Finally, always remember the golden rule in the circle for both attackers and defenders: always follow the shot in case it misses – rebounds represent a second chance! Take every opportunity to reaffirm this and form good habits.

Objective: To introduce and practise the correct shooting action and technique.

Equipment: One post, one ball between two players.

Description: The shooter shoots for goal from various positions in the circle area, starting close to the post and gradually moving further away. Her partner retrieves the ball and returns it to the shooter using a chest pass. After 10 shots swap roles.

Coaching points: Look for the correct shooting action – see the introduction to this section. Encourage the shooter to adopt a balanced position and controlled shooting action. The accuracy comes from the balance of the shooter and the timing of the pass combined with the wrist snap and leg push. Encourage the shooter to aim for the back of the ring. Look for a good-quality chest pass from the retriever.

Progression: The shooter starts with her back to the post. When the feeder shouts 'Go' she quickly turns to face the feeder, receives a pass and then shoots.

drill 77 *shooting relay*

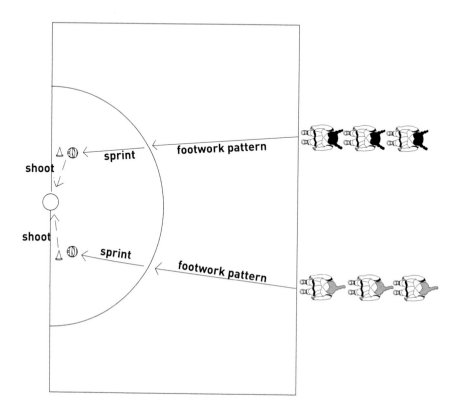

shoot

sprint

footwork pattern

shoot

sprint

footwork pattern

Objective: To practise getting into a balanced position to shoot following a move into the circle.

Equipment: Two balls, two cones and one goalpost. Players in two teams.

Description: The balls are placed at the cones, which are placed in the circle in a good shooting position. One at a time from each team, players move towards the circle edge using different movement patterns. They then sprint to the cone, pick up the ball and either score a goal or have a maximum of three shots at goal. They then pass the ball to the next player on their team, who should have reached the circle edge and then sprinted into the circle to receive the pass. The first player goes to the back of their team. Each player needs to complete three trips to the post. The first team to finish is the winner.

Coaching points: Look for balanced, controlled movement into the circle and a balanced shooting action.

Progression: Add a defender. Add a feeder to pass the ball to the shooters.

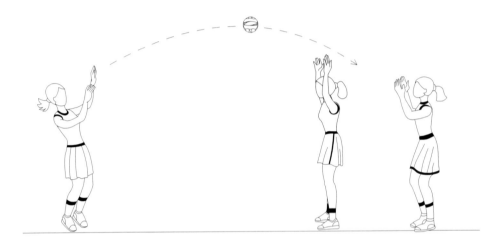

Objective: To practise holding the space behind a player to receive an overhead pass. This can be used under the post or on backline or sideline throw-ins.

Equipment: One ball between three players.

Description: One player is the feeder, one is the attacker and one is the defender. The feeder starts with the ball (this position would be WA, GA or C in a game). The attacker stands behind the defender, slightly sideways, with one foot behind the other, and indicates to receive the ball behind her. The feeder should throw an over-head pass to land behind the attacker, who should hold her position until the ball is overhead and then take one step back to catch the ball.

Coaching points: The attacker should use her body to shield the space in which she wants to receive the ball from the defender. If the attacker moves backwards too early the defender will be able to step back and make an easy interception.

Progression: Vary the position of the feeder so the attacker has to receive the pass from different directions.

drill 79 jump and shoot

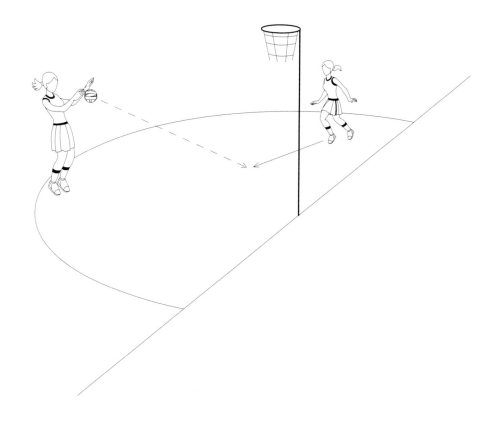

Objective: To practise controlling forward movement, getting into a balanced shooting position and maintaining correct shooting action technique.

Equipment: One ball and one goalpost between two players.

Description: One player is shooting, the other is the feeder, standing on the circle edge. The shooter starts on the opposite side of the circle just inside the circle edge, facing the post. When ready, the shooter sprints into the space underneath the post and the feeder passes her the ball. The shooter should jump to catch the ball and land two-footed, then attempt a shot.

Coaching points: Look for a fast, controlled sprint into a space by the shooter and a balanced, two-footed landing. The shooter only has five seconds to shoot once she has received the ball, so the more accurate the pass and the more controlled the landing the better. Look for correct shooting technique and a balanced shooting position.

Progression: Vary the starting positions of the feeder and shooter.

drill 80 under the post

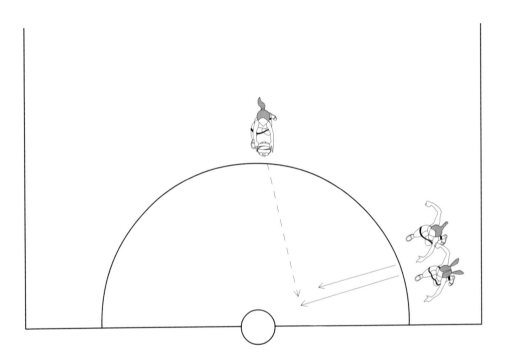

Objective: To practise getting free of a defender to receive the ball under the post.

Equipment: One ball and one goalpost between three players.

Description: Divide the players into groups of three. The feeder stands on the circle edge with the ball. The shooter and defender start opposite the feeder, with the defender between the ball and the shooter. The shooter sprints into the space under the post to receive the ball, aiming to get there before the defender. The defender can try to intercept the ball or tip it to prevent the shooter receiving the ball.

Coaching points: Look for a fast, controlled sprint by the shooter. The defender can hold back at first if the shooter is having difficulty receiving the pass.

Progression: Introduce a dodge for the shooter to get free of the defender and move into a space under the post.

drill 81 rebound

Objective: To develop awareness and control of space in the circle.

Equipment: One ball between three players in the shooting circle.

Description: Two shooters stand in the circle. The feeder stands on the circle edge with the ball. The shooters dodge to get free and the feeder passes to each one in turn. The shooter then assumes a good shooting position and makes the shot, following the ball. The second shooter takes control of the space under the post, waiting for the rebound and preventing her imaginary defender from gaining access to this vital space. Shooters score one point for every successful shot and two points for every rebound caught. After each shot or rebound the ball is returned to the feeder.

Coaching points: Look for confident dodges into space and shooters holding space to receive a pass. Shooters should aim to receive the pass close to the post. Encourage shooters to follow every shot with their hands ready to catch the rebound.

Progression: Add defenders to mark the shooters. The feeder may choose to pass to whichever shooter is in the best position.

drill 82 *rolling attack*

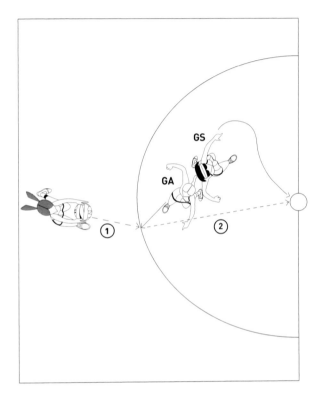

Objective: To improve communication between GA and GS.

Equipment: One ball and a goalpost between three players.

Description: Start off with GA and GS together in the heart of the circle. GA runs to receive a pass at the edge of the circle while GS 'rolls' off around the (imaginary) defender to take up a shooting position at the post. GA passes to GS, who shoots.

Coaching points: GS will be able to see what space GA takes up and should respond accordingly. Ensure that all movements are decisive and strong.

Progression: The first pass can be received at different points of the circle, and GS has to respond accordingly. Once the drill has been mastered add a defender.

GAME SCENARIOS

These drills cover typical game situations and introduce some basic tactics of netball to players with some understanding of the game and who need to develop their skills. The drills will give players some experience of coping with different scenarios and trying out different options to outmanoeuvre their opponents.

The drills also include the development of quick reactions and practice of decision making in different game situations with options for centre passes, throw-ins, and attacking and defensive sequences.

Aim to keep the practices simple at the start; try to limit the number of things you are asking players to remember. Encourage them to try out different positions to help them understand the roles and responsibilities of each position and decide which position they prefer or are better suited to through experience. This also helps develop good team spirit!

the centre pass

Younger or inexperienced players can adopt a very regimented approach to starting the game and the centre pass, standing in the same position on the third line every time, moving the same way and throwing the ball to the same person. The player in the centre position has the pressure of starting the game for her team and often looks to pass to her friend or loudest player on court.

The rule for the start of the game is that all players must be on-side, i.e. standing behind the third line in the attacking or defensive third area with the centre making the pass from the centre circle. It doesn't matter where the GA, WA or GD and WD actually stand in their respective third – in fact as they become more skilled and experienced an option is to keep moving away from their defender before the centre pass is made. This does require confidence and the ability to make quick decisions – a skill younger and inexperienced players need to develop over time.

Encourage players to try out different places on the third line to start the game to help develop awareness of their options and build the confidence to assert where they want to start the game, or to cope if their defender does something they haven't come across before. This is particularly important if the centre pass isn't going well – starting in a different place can confuse the defender and help make some space to run in to.

Coaching points:

1 Obviously the centre pass is crucial to start the game play and keep possession. Young players often feel a lot of pressure, especially the centre; coaches should stress that all centre court players have responsibility for the centre pass going well. The centre must make a quick decision about who to pass to and make a

direct, accurate pass and the WA, GA, GD and WD have responsibility to get free from their defenders to receive the pass.

2   GA and WA should try to get into position along their third line approximately 3 m from the sideline on the outside of their defender. This gives them space away from their defender to run in to and receive a pass without being blocked in by the sideline.

3   Defenders cannot mark with their arms across the front of the body of their attackers and cannot lean on their attacker.

4   Encourage a straight, direct pass from the centre – a looped pass is slower and easier to intercept.

It can help for a team to work to an agreed pattern at the centre pass so players know where the ball is going next. This can be two passes to the WA, one to the GA, two to the WD and so on – or any particular combination. Or the centre can give a secret signal to indicate who will receive the next pass. Working to a signal or agreed pattern has the advantage of introducing an order for players to work to, taking away the unpredictability. Take care though – it can also create too rigid a structure for players to rely on, which restricts their ability to think quickly and decide what to do if they face a new situation. Remember, opponents don't always do what you expect and will have their own tactics to try and put you off!

With both players concentrating on the ball, Jade Clarke of England is challenged by Temepara George of New Zealand who avoids contacting Jade by using the arm furthest away from her opponent to try to intercept the ball.

drill 83 attacking centre pass

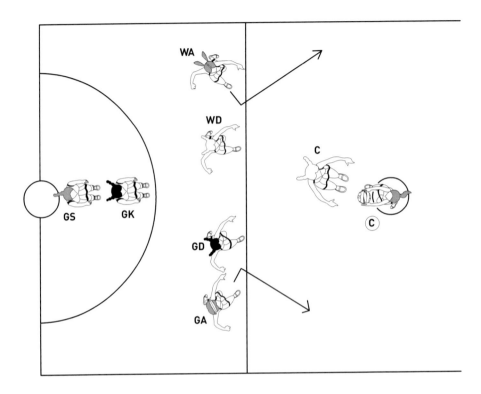

Objective: To practise dodging to get free and receive the centre pass.

Equipment: One ball and half the court between eight players.

Description: This drill allows players to practise an alternative way of getting free for the centre pass than a simple straight run to the side. On the coach's whistle, the WA and GA dodge to get free and sprint into the centre third. The defenders should stand still at first. The pass can go to either player, as chosen by the C (for younger players the coach may need to indicate where the pass should go at first).

Coaching points: The dodge should be a definite movement: controlled, quick and balanced. Look for the WA and GA pushing off on their outside foot and using their shoulders to help feign the dodge and make the move quick and controlled.

Progression: Introduce the defenders. Encourage them to try to stick with their attacking partners and intercept the ball.

drill 84 *centre pass using WD and GD*

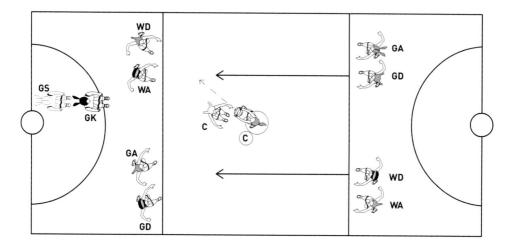

Objective: To practise WD/GD receiving a centre pass in an attacking position.

Equipment: One ball and half the court between 12 players.

Description: Set up the players as shown. C starts with the ball and should be facing away from the WD and GD. On the coach's whistle, WD and GD sprint forwards in a straight line, aiming to receive the ball as close to the attacking third line as possible. Alternate the players receiving the pass. Restrict defending players (WA and GA) until the WD and GD are more confident.

Coaching points: To receive a centre pass without the ball being intercepted, the WD and GD should position themselves inside their defending players ready for the centre pass. It is worth letting WD and GD try to receive the centre pass having started on the outside of their defending players – this puts the C under more pressure to make an accurate pass and makes it easier for WA and GA to intercept the ball.

Progression: Encourage the defending players to try for the interception. Look for the player receiving the pass to make a second pass to either the WA or GA.

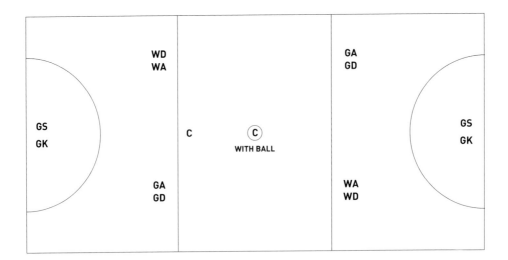

Objective: To practise defending a centre pass to put pressure on the attacking team.

Equipment: Full court, centre court players, one ball.

Description: The defending team practise trying to force the attacking players out of position for their centre pass by manoeuvring their attacking players to the inside – as shown in the diagram. The defending C takes up position in between the players to further reduce the space the WA or GA have to run into. The GA and WA of the defending team also try and block their players into a small space as shown – this reduces the space they have to run into to try and receive the centre pass. Run through some centre passes and let the players try out different moves to try and block their players and restrict their movement.

Coaching points: The defending players can block their players from moving into more space – look out for contact. Players must still avoid contact in this situation. To start, and to let the defenders get a feel of the pincer movement, the attackers should set up in the positions shown in the diagram. As players get used to how this affects the play, encourage the attackers to try and get into a position of choice for the centre pass and for the defender to try and block them in the positions as shown. For the attackers, encourage them to keep moving to avoid being blocked into a position with limited space to move.

the throw-in

The next set of drills will help develop good technique when taking and receiving throw-ins from various positions on court. Who takes the throw-in depends on where on the court the ball goes out of play. The following drills show typical positions for a throw-in on the court. Younger players don't always think about positioning and spacing on court and are keen to take throw-ins to be part of the game wherever they may be. However, if the player taking the throw-in is out of position on the court, this can have a negative impact on the next sequence of passes in the game. Encouraging young players to think about the 'correct' person to take the throw-in is a good habit to get into.

The following drills enable players to practise set moves for a variety of throw-ins, although the combinations are endless and players will need to be encouraged to be flexible and think about the best options available in each situation.

Coaching points to consider when taking a throw-in

1 When taking a throw-in, the player must stand with one foot up to – but not touching – the line of the court. This indicates to the umpire that the player is ready to make the pass. If the player's feet are touching the line, a free throw-in will be given to the opposite team. An umpire may also penalise a player who is standing too far away from the line – this is not likely to happen with younger players, but good positioning is a good habit to get into.
2 The player taking the throw-in should look to pass the ball into an attacking or forward position on court. There may be occasions when the throw-in will need to be passed backwards if players are not free, but players should be encouraged to look forwards.
3 All players must be on court before the pass is taken. This also applies to members of the opposite team, who may have gone off court to retrieve the ball. If a player takes the throw-in without waiting for that player to be on court, a free pass will be given to the opposite team.
4 Players on court should be ready to receive the pass, either holding a space to run into or ready to dodge and get free.
5 Players defending a throw-in should be 1 m away from the line to avoid giving away a penalty pass.
6 Any backline throw-in taken in the defence goal third should be taken by the GK.
7 Never throw a backline pass across the circle – if the pass is intercepted, this gives the attacking team an immediate shot at goal.

The player taking the throw-in can decide whether to take the throw-in quickly or take more time. There may be an advantage gained if the throw-in is taken quickly – for example to get the ball into the circle to an unmarked GA or GS. There may also be advantages to taking more time to prepare before taking the throw-in – for example if team players are out of position and need time to recover on court.

throw-in from the backline – in the circle

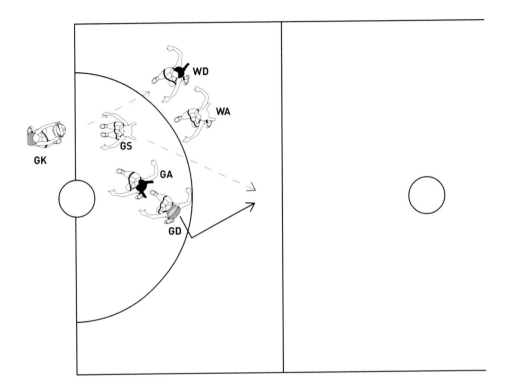

Objective: To practise WD and GD receiving a backline throw-in in the circle.

Equipment: One ball and half the court between five players.

Description: The defensive backline pass will always be taken by the GK, where-ever the ball goes out of court. The GK starts with the ball standing on the back-line. The other players start in the positions shown. WD and GD hold their position on the circle edge – making it harder for the WA and GA to mark them. When ready, the GK should step up to the line as if to take the throw-in, which is the indication to the other players that she/he is ready. The WD or GD is going to receive the pass at the circle edge, shielding the ball from the WA or GA with her body. Alternatively, the WD or GD can dodge to get free. Alternate passes to WD and GD.

Coaching points: Encourage the WD and GD to hold the space on the edge of the circle. Any movement before the pass will give an advantage to the defender.

Progression: The GD or WD – depending on who receives the first ball – should be ready for the next pass.

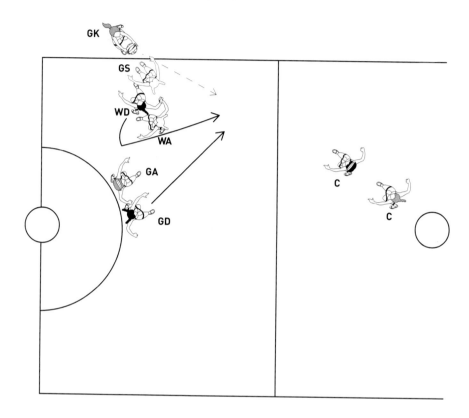

Objective: To practise a sideline throw-in in the defensive third.

Equipment: One ball and half the court between eight players.

Description: The GK should take the throw-in. The WD or GD should aim to receive the pass. WD and GD should dodge to get free of their marker or hold a space to run into. Alternate passes to WD and GD. If WD receives the throw-in, the GD should move for the next pass and vice versa.

Coaching points: Encourage communication between the players. Players should hold their space and resist moving up the court to help receive the pass – this causes crowding.

Progression: The GK decides which player to pass to depending on who is in the best position to receive the pass.

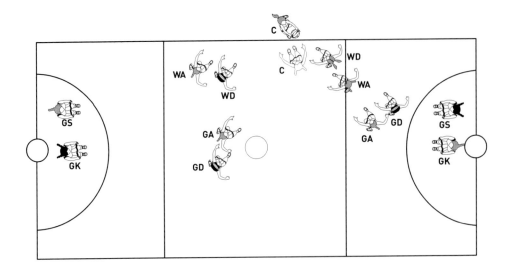

Objective: To practise a throw-in in the centre court. The aim is to encourage players to decide who will receive the throw-in and avoid crowding around the ball.

Equipment: One ball and the full court.

Description: The coach should vary the position of the throw-in. Let the players play out the sideline pass aiming to maintain an attacking position.

Coaching points: The coach must ensure that a clear pass is given to a player and that the player receiving the throw-in makes a definite move to receive the ball. Other players should avoid crowding and look to receive the next pass. Encourage lots of communication and stop the drill if players do crowd the ball. Walk the players through the possible moves if needed.

Progression: Vary the player taking the throw-in and receiving the pass. Encourage the players to take responsibility for deciding who will take the throw-in and receive the pass rather than the coach dictating this all the time.

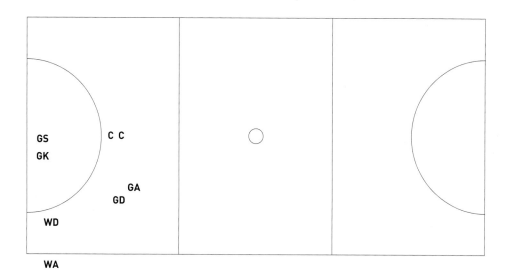

Objective: To practise defending a throw-in in the goal third to put pressure on the attacking team.

Equipment: One ball, eight players, goal third.

Description: The attacking team have a throw-in on the sideline close to the circle or the backline. The defending team try to put pressure on the attacking team to reduce the space they have to move into or to make an accurate pass. The attacking team must try and score a goal.

Coaching points: The WA or C would take this throw-in to leave the GA and GS free to get into a good position to score a goal. The key to defending a throw-in when it is close to the circle is to defend the circle edge – as shown with the WD taking position close to the circle to cut off a direct pass into the GA or GS. This also defends the space preventing the GA moving into the circle on this side. Holding this position on the circle edge reduces passing and moving options for the attacking team. The player on the circle edge should have high arms to further reduce the sight into the circle of the player taking the throw-in. GK and GD should aim to get between their player and the ball. The attacking C should try to move into a space at the top of the circle, closest to the ball – the defending C should aim to prevent this, forcing the C as far away from the sideline as possible – this forces a long pass from the WA if the only option she has is to pass to her C, which may be easier to intercept.

Pamela Cookey of England and Rebecca Bulley of Australia contest for the ball under the post showing the physical skills and determination needed in netball.

CONDITIONED GAMES

Young players not only have to learn the basic skills of netball (balance, control, passing and catching techniques, footwork etc.) they also have to learn the roles and responsibilities of the seven team positions and be able to understand sufficiently to put all this into practice in a game. This is a challenge even for players who have played some netball and they still need lots of support, encouragement and praise to help them develop these skills.

There can be a tendency for players to revert back to old habits when playing in a game rather than trying newly coached skills or techniques; even if you have just delivered a highly successful coaching session incorporating well-structured drills! Conditioned games provide an opportunity for players and coaches to put the new skills and techniques into practice in a game situation. For this to be fully effective the coach must make sure that the objective and the link between the drill and the game are very clear and understood – ask the players to help make this link. Without this understanding there is a tendency for a conditioned game to turn into a run-around with lots of frustration!

When players are under pressure, faced with defenders and limited time to choose and make their pass, with teammates calling out for the ball to be passed to them, the easy, safe option is to hurl the ball any which way and get rid of it! The drills they have just run through are long forgotten.

Enthusiasm can often get the better of players too, with everyone running after the ball, shouting at teammates and with little regard for positions on the court, spacing and control.

To encourage players (of all ages and abilities) to practise using the skills you have drilled during coaching sessions in a game situation it sometimes helps to make the new skill or technique a condition in the game, with a failure to use or apply this rule resulting in a free pass to the opponents.

The following drills are suggestions for conditioned games that I have found particularly helpful for younger, inexperienced players to help them develop their netballing skills and improve their understanding of the role of the positions and spacing on court.

Coaching points:

1 Link the condition in the game to the drills that have been practised as part of the training session – the idea is to encourage players to try out their new skills.
2 Only apply one condition at a time for young players – don't give them too much extra to think about, as this will only confuse things.
3 Use conditioned games for a short time to avoid frustration building when trying to learn something new.
4 Encourage players to spot when the skills and techniques have been used – this is useful for players waiting to join in the game and for players on the court – extra points can be awarded if the team spots when the condition has been correctly applied.

drill 90 *space out!*

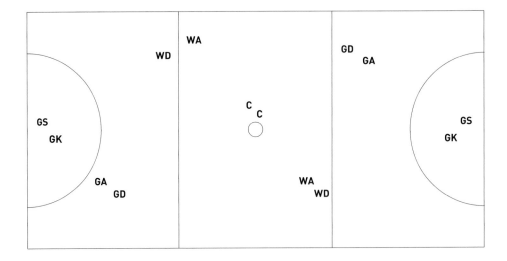

Objective: To encourage players to be more aware of their main area of responsibility and the space on the court. Particularly aimed at GA and GD to prevent them hovering out of position at their opposite third line.

Description: GA and GD on each team are restricted to their goal third and not allowed to move into the centre third to receive a pass apart from the centre pass. The condition here is that they play in the same area as GS and GK.

Coaching points: This helps to keep players evenly spaced throughout the court and prevents GA or GD being out of position in moving up to their opposite third line when the opposing team are attacking or defending. This means the GA will always be in her attacking third when the ball is being moved into attack – important as she is one of only two shooters! When a backline pass is being taken from the defending team, or following an interception, encourage passes to be made in sequence through the team positions: GK to GD or WD, to C, to WA then GA, as the ball moves up the court towards the circle. Defenders should be making and receiving passes in the defending half, attackers in the attacking half.

drill 91 get free!

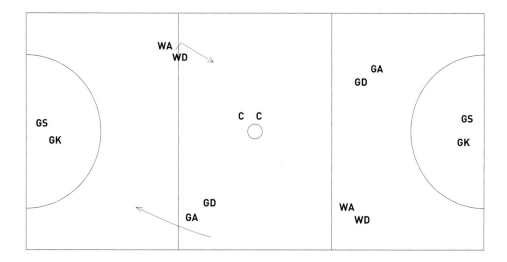

Objective: To encourage players to dodge and get free of their defender to receive a pass.

Description: All passes in a game to be a chest pass.

Coaching points: Remind players that a chest pass is aimed at short distances and look for good chest passing technique. Encourage players to make a dodge and move forwards towards the player with the ball to receive the pass. The condition can be relaxed for passes into the circle – unless you want to encourage the GS and GA to move forward to receive their pass.

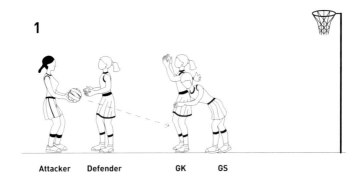

1

Attacker   Defender   GK   GS

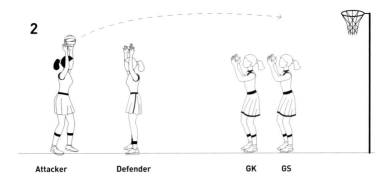

2

Attacker   Defender   GK   GS

Objective: To encourage players to practise a bounce or lob pass into the circle to avoid the defenders.

Description: All passes made into the circle to a GA or GS to be a bounce or lob pass. Pick one pass as the condition for inexperienced players – for more experienced players both types of pass can be applied.

Coaching points: Look for good passing technique. For a lob pass encourage the GS and GA to hold their space under the post and stand still until the ball is overhead. Encourage them to jump to catch the ball out of the air and not to move too soon which will make it easier for the defenders to intercept the ball. For defenders, encourage them to mark their shooter closely and try to keep them as far from the post as possible. WD and C should also try and mark their opponents closely to make it harder for them to make an accurate pass.

drill 93 arms up!

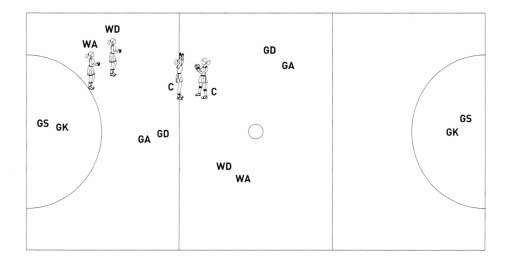

Objective: To encourage players to defend when their opponent has the ball, and to increase awareness of when a situation in a game moves from attack to defence.

Description: Players must mark their opponent facing towards them with their arms up when their opposing team player has the ball. The aim is for them to make it as difficult as possible for the player to make an accurate pass.

Coaching points: Look for the correct distance when marking the player with the ball to avoid a penalty pass being awarded. Encourage players to quickly move to defending the ball and encourage teammates to do the same, for example after an interception when one team will be moving from defending to attacking.

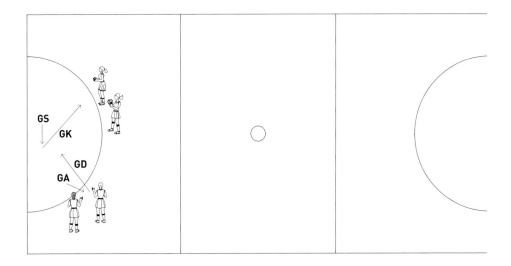

Objective: To encourage GS and GA to move in the circle to get free for a pass and get free from the defenders.

Description: Before the GA or GS can make a shot they have to pass the ball back out of the circle to their WA or C and receive a second pass. The second pass into the circle doesn't have to go to the same player.

Coaching points: This prevents shooters being lazy and just trying to hold their space under the post. This works against some defenders, but a shooter always needs an alternative. Encourage the shooters to keep moving in the circle to confuse their defender. Defenders should try and limit this movement by blocking the space – only focus on this type of defence for more experienced players; look for close marking from less confident defenders and build up to the blocking. To gain advantage, the pass back out of the circle should be quick – players need to be ready. Encourage players to experiment with their passes and movement to see which works the best.

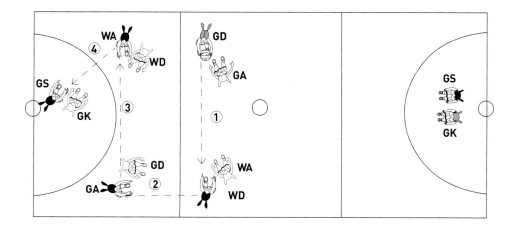

Objective: To encourage players to move to receive a pass, to keep moving to make space if the first move is not successful and move towards the player with the ball.

Description: Play a normal game with the condition that players are not able to pass the ball to the player they received the ball from.

Coaching points: This condition emphasises the need to be constantly moving to make a space to move into to receive a pass. It also helps involve more players and avoids a chain of two or three linking to move the ball around the court. Encourage a player to make second and third moves if they are not successful. Look for dodges and balanced movements with good indication (pointing to where they are moving) to the thrower of where they want to receive the pass.

drill 96 *silence*

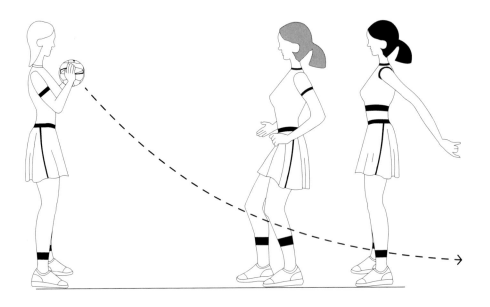

Objective: To encourage players to react to the game situation and learn the importance of all types of communication between team members in a game.

Description: Play a normal game with the condition that players are not able to call out for the ball. Players should use hand and eye signals to indicate where they want to receive a pass, or show where they are moving to.

Coaching points: This condition emphasises the need for good communication on court and being aware of where team members are – temporarily removing the ability for them to shout out will help to show how important being able to give clear verbal signals is in a game. Keep these games short to avoid frustration building – silence is not a normal situation and although conversation on court is not what you are looking for, players do need to be able to call out to each other.

WARMING DOWN

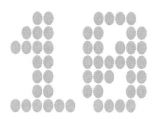

At the end of the session the players will be hot and probably tired. It is a mistake to just say, 'Thanks for coming' and let them wander off. Instead, always perform a warm-down to finish each session. This will provide a number of important functions:

- The warm-down is a great opportunity to work on flexibility as the muscles are warm.
- The warm-down allows the body to begin to flush out many of the waste products produced during vigorous exercise.
- The warm-down represents the 'bracket' to the session and will ensure that players feel that this was a well-thought-out, well-structured session, which all adds to the atmosphere of excellence and care that will motivate a group to work effectively.

Just as with all the drills in this book, the warm-down sessions must focus on form; only strict form will provide the intended benefits.

drill 97 hamstring reach

Objective: To warm down the body and to improve flexibility.

Equipment: One ball per player.

Description: Line the players up along the baseline with feet wider than shoulder width apart and the ball between their feet. On the coach's command, the players reach down (keeping their legs straight at all times), pick up the ball and place it as far back through their legs as they can. The player then walks backwards until their feet are in line with the ball and repeats the drill. The aim is to cover the given distance (approximately 10 m) in as few pick-ups as possible.

Coaching points: Watch for cheats who bend their legs to gain an advantage! Remind them that this is a slow, controlled race and form is everything.

drill 98 *side stretch*

Objective: To warm down the body and improve flexibility.

Equipment: One ball per player.

Description: Line the players up with their right side facing into court, feet wider than shoulder width apart, legs straight and the ball in front of their left foot. On the coach's command, the players bend down (keeping their legs straight), pick up the ball and place it in front of their right foot. Then, leaving the ball where it is, the players swap feet, progressing into the court, so that the ball is by their left foot once more. The movement is then repeated for a set distance – 10 m is more than enough for this drill.

Coaching points: Watch for cheats who bend their legs to gain an advantage! Reiterate that the movements should be slow and controlled, keeping perfect form.

drill 99 *circle stretch 1*

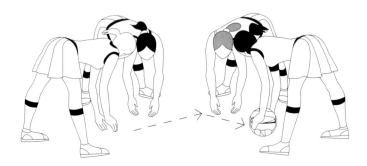

Objective: To warm down the body and improve flexibility.

Equipment: One ball between four players.

Description: Form the players into a circle with their feet wider than shoulder width apart, and their feet touching those of the next players (i.e. right foot to left foot). Keeping the legs straight, all the players reach down and hang their hands as close to the floor as possible. The ball is rolled from one player to another around the circle. After 10 passes in total, walk the players around for a minute and then repeat.

Coaching points: Watch for cheats who bend their legs to gain an advantage!

Progression: If you have enough players, form two or more groups and race them to see who is first to complete the passes.

drill 100 *circle stretch 2*

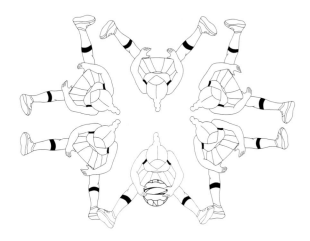

Objective: To warm down the body and improve flexibility.

Equipment: One ball between six players.

Description: Sit the players back to back in a circle with their legs wide apart and feet touching. The ball is passed in order around the circle. Each player must give and take the ball with two hands every time.

Coaching points: This drill provides a stretch to the backs of the legs and requires good flexibility, as each player must rotate the trunk to make the pass. If players lack flexibility, they will creep their bottoms away from the group so that they are leaning back rather than sitting upright. Try to keep the legs nice and straight throughout.

Progression: If you have enough players, form two or more groups and race to see who is the first to complete the passes. Vary the direction of passing on command.

drill 101 *giant strides*

Objective: To warm down the body and improve flexibility.

Equipment: Cones.

Description: Players line up facing into court. Mark out a line about 10 m away using the cones. Keeping the body upright, each player takes a slow, controlled stride forwards. The stride should be as long as possible without losing control. Repeat over the set distance then walk the players back to the start. Repeat.

Coaching points: This drill only works if the body is strictly upright with a 'proud' chest and the head up. In effect, it is an exaggerated running stride. The more slowly this drill is performed, the better. The challenge is for each player to beat her own standards – if she can cover the distance in five strides, she should try to cover it in four and a half next time, and so on.